WICCAPEDIA

WICCAPEDIA

A MODERN-DAY
WHITE WITCH'S GUIDE

SHAWN
ROBBINS

LEANNA
GREENAWAY

STERLING ETHOS
New York

STERLING ETHOS
New York

An Imprint of Sterling Publishing Co., Inc.
1166 Avenue of the Americas
New York, NY 10036

This new edition published by Sterling Publishing Co., Inc., in 2014.
Previously published in 2011 by Sterling Publishing Co., Inc., in a different format.

A full list of picture credits appears on page 296 at the back of the book.

ISBN 978-1-4549-1374-0

Library of Congress Cataloging-in-Publication Data

Robbins, Shawn.
  Wiccapedia : a modern-day white witch's guide / Shawn Robbins & Leanna Greenaway.
    p. cm.
  Includes index.
  ISBN 978-1-4027-7724-0 (pb-trade pbk.) 1. Witchcraft. I. Greenaway, Leanna. II. Title.
  BF1566.R55 2011
  133.4'3--dc22

                      2010046594

Distributed in Canada by Sterling Publishing Co., Inc.
c/o Canadian Manda Group, 664 Annette Street
Toronto, Ontario, Canada M6S 2C8
Distributed in the United Kingdom by GMC Distribution Services
Castle Place, 166 High Street, Lewes, East Sussex, England BN7 1XU
Distributed in Australia by NewSouth Books
45 Beach Street, Coogee, NSW 2034, Australia

For information about custom editions, special sales, and premium and corporate purchases,
please contact Sterling Special Sales at 800-805-5489 or specialsales@sterlingpublishing.com.

Manufactured in the United States of America

8 10 9 7

www.sterlingpublishing.com

In memory of my mom, who taught me to soar above the clouds and reach for the impossible dream.

—*Shawn Robbins*

To my mother, Beleta Greenaway, who has had her brains picked to the limit once again. You are my inspiration and my muse; thank you, Mamma.

—*Leanna Greenaway*

DISCLAIMER

This book is designed to educate and entertain while providing information regarding the subject matter covered. It is sold with the understanding that the publishers and authors are not thereby engaged in rendering legal, medical, or any other professional services. If such services are required, the services of a competent professional should be sought. Some countries may have regulations that prohibit the use of terms or performance of actions discussed in this book. In these cases the reader is urged to comply with such regulations.

Every effort has been made to ensure that this book is as complete and as accurate as possible within the space available. However, there may be mistakes, both typographical and in content, and additionally, the book contains only information available to the authors up to the date of first publication. Therefore the text should be used only as a general guide and not as the ultimate source of information on the subjects covered.

The purpose of this book is to entertain and inform. The authors and the publishers shall have neither liability nor responsibility to any person or entity with respect to any loss or damage caused, directly or indirectly, by the information contained in this book.

CONTENTS

PART FOUR

PSYCHIC ABILITY AND DIVINATION

APPENDIX I

APPENDIX II

AUTHORS' NOTE

SHAWN ROBBINS

I am a mischievous psychic witch on the American side of the pond who is just coming out of the broom closet. To me, being a Wiccan is a way of life. It's a belief that all things are magickal and that you have the power within yourself to change the world around you for the better, including your own world. It's the freedom to go out in the darkest hours of the night and wish upon a shining star that your hopes and dreams come true. It's the desire to share with others how being a Wiccan, as I have learned, can turn your weaknesses into strengths. Wicca can help you live life to the fullest, and in this book we will show you how to combine the extraordinary tools of Wicca with the powers of psychic intuition that we all have within us. I don't expect or want everybody to be deeply psychic like me. I just want everyone to be their own personal best, learning by example and sharing those experiences with others. My coauthor, Leanna Greenaway, told me to embrace who I am and not be afraid of what the world thinks. Her words were the inspiration that brought me out of the broom closet and into the world—and what a relief!

You see, from the time I was a very young child, I knew I had a different way of seeing the world around me. Not only could I see what others couldn't, but I could also hear, feel, and sense things that weren't apparent to my friends. Some people might think of this as a burden, especially for a child, but I never did. I knew that this "gift" ran in my family, and that my grandmother, in particular, was highly in tune with her sixth (and maybe seventh, eighth, and ninth) sense. I was never frightened by my abilities, never wished I didn't have them. They were always just a part of me, as natural to me as breathing the fresh air.

One thing I can say about being a psychic child is that there were few surprises. I always knew what the Hanukkah Santa was going to bring me. I knew when my friends were going to call or pop by; I knew when my parents tried to plan surprise parties for me. But since I'm curious by nature, I didn't consider these insights to be "spoilers"—I loved knowing what no one else seemed to, and because I was so young, the fact that it frustrated some people only made it more enjoyable to me!

Even when my visions were of impending danger, I didn't shrink from them or try to close them out of my mind. In fact, my first premonition occurred when I was a very little girl, and it woke me out of a sound sleep. I was screaming, "Fire! Fire! Daddy!" and I felt as though I were choking. My mother ran to my side and tried to calm me, but I was having none of that, and I kept on screaming. Well, she happened to turn her head to look into the living room, where my father had fallen asleep, and saw that there was something smoldering. An electrical wire had become exposed and started to burn its way through the rug. When the danger had passed, I realized (with great relief) that I had probably saved my family and that I needed to pay attention to my visions in the future.

I've had some amazing opportunities to use my gifts for the greater good over the years. I have found many different ways to provide information to people who are looking for something *more*. And I am happy to do it, because I feel that—although I didn't ask for it—when I was *given* the gift of seeing, I was also given a responsibility to *give back*.

Let me back up for a moment and tell you about my family. My mom was born in 1918 and was just eleven years old when the Great Depression hit in

1929—old enough to realize how bad things really were, yet young enough to feel completely helpless about it. Fortunately, my mother had a knack for fortune-telling, and she read palms during those difficult years for seekers who could spare a dime.

Like most of the women in my family, my mother had a way of looking for the positive in any situation, even when it was extremely difficult to find. As a young woman, my poor, penniless mom treasured the cardboard "shoes" she made from boxes. She would put those boxes on her feet and think of them as her magickal slippers, dreaming that they would take her to far-flung places—anywhere other than where she was, practically homeless and struggling to survive from day to day. This is an important story, I think, because it's very typical of people who have otherworldly senses. Psychics have a way of losing themselves in the possibilities that life has to offer. We wonder what the future holds: how our lives might change, what we might be like a year or two from now. This is why we're sometimes called flighty and flaky, but there's a good reason for it. We tend not to dwell on what is— especially if we're stuck in a less-than-desirable situation—because we know (and I mean we *know* with absolute certainty) that something better is always coming up around the bend.

That's what I learned from my mom. She taught me that hope is never futile or silly, that daring to dream of a better tomorrow is the only way to live. She instilled in me the belief that although not everyone is fortunate in this life, there are ways to help people find their way through the muck and the mire. Giving is the way to inner happiness, both for you and for the person you're giving to. That's what my mother believed, and that's what I try to do with my life—help people find answers: for those who are simply curious; for those who have lost their way; or for those who are deep in despair, convinced that nothing good is out there waiting for them. Fortune-telling is, for me, a way to give people hope when they may not have any, even if that means I have to search out that one little positive thing that's coming their way. We all need a small ray of light to keep us going. Sometimes that's all there is. If I can expose it—hand someone a pair of virtual sunglasses and honestly say, "The future is bright, my friend!"—I consider that a success.

The upside of this is that I can really have a hand in helping people to be the best that they can be. Without hope, there is nothing. Someone who has no faith in the future isn't going to use their own gifts to better themselves or the world around them—and what a loss that could be for all of us! The downside of my abilities is more personal. Psychics naturally tend to be very empathetic (in fact, many of us are empaths—that is, we can literally feel the energy of others), and we also tend to be altruistic. We can't bear to see suffering, because we feel as if we should be able to help. We've been given these amazing abilities and we want to use them to fix everyone and everything! Of course, that's just not possible. For every one person I know I've helped, there are others still out there in need of help—people living on the street, sick people in hospitals, hungry children. So we look for other ways to help. We donate—money, time, whatever we have. Outside the setting of a formal reading, sometimes just in passing conversations, we try to pass on positive energy by encouraging others to be optimistic and selfless. It's who we are, as a group, and it's what we can do.

Personally, I want to reach out and mentor people to be their very best. I don't mean that they have to be wealthy or famous or extraordinary by society's standards. I want to see them recognize the goodness inside of themselves, all that life has to offer them, and the different ways that they can be shining stars to others. If I can do that, then I consider my work done—and done well.

LEANNA GREENAWAY

I was born and grew up in England. From about the age of four or five, I guess I knew I was different from the other kids in kindergarten. They would sit at their desks singing some nursery rhyme or other and looking adoringly at the teacher. Me? Well, I was daydreaming, looking out the window and wondering how I could get Jesus to play hopscotch with me at recess. I believed that he was by my side every minute of every day, mainly because there was this mysterious white light in my peripheral vision that would just appear when I least expected it. At times, it would remain there for an hour; other times, it would linger for a day or two. In my naïveté I assumed that this bodiless light was in fact Jesus, probably because, back then, school assemblies were filled with prayers and hymns and most Christian kids went to Sunday school as a matter of course.

When I look back now, I know that my "mysterious light," which tagged along with me for most of my childhood, was probably my guide or angel.

As a child, I thought everyone saw this strange light out of the corner of their eye. I didn't speak about it to anyone, mainly because I thought it was perfectly normal to see it. I asked a few friends in primary school about their lights, and they had no idea what I was talking about! I think that I just had an innate understanding of the spirit world without ever being told about it. However, this prompted many questions, and I began to explore my spirituality and look for guidance.

My parents weren't religious, nor were they churchgoers—far from it. I went to Sunday school with my best friend, Lorraine, every week for about two years. Her father would take us on a motorbike with a sidecar, and for me there was nothing better than the ride in that cranky piece of metal, complete with goggles on my nose, a 1970s purple crash helmet on my head, and the wind blowing in my face. It was such a treat.

At the tender age of seven, I was sitting in church one Sunday, listening to the reverend talk about the Bible, when suddenly it dawned on me that the sermon he was giving didn't ring true to my soul. Even at such a young age, I was quite grown-up and pragmatic, and I began to question the Bible stories. I couldn't for the life of me get how Jesus could walk on water! One day, I innocently asked the reverend in front of the entire congregation whether Jesus was in fact walking on ice. Maybe, I suggested, the author of the Bible had left that part out accidentally. It seemed perfectly plausible to me that some freak storm had caused the Sea of Galilee to freeze over and that was how he had managed to do it, but to just magickally tiptoe over the water— no, I didn't buy it! A rather plump lady with an ample bosom and a big hat swiftly ushered me out for asking too many questions.

The incident stayed on my mind, though, and because I was never given any logical answers, I began searching for my own explanations.

My mother started to explore her own spirituality only because she had a little dark-haired witch of a daughter who would question her relentlessly about things she didn't understand. She would come into my room to kiss me goodnight and find me sitting cross-legged on the bed, meditating. When she asked me what I was doing, I would say that I was looking for my pretty lights. When I was about ten, I started hearing voices in my head. Sometimes there were too many all chatting away at once, and I would hold my hands over my ears and beg to make them stop. But the voices didn't go away, and as I reached adolescence, it was clear that I had tapped into some kind of extrasensory portal and was showing signs of being mediumistic.

I was like a little psychic time bomb about to go off, and as I grew, so did my gift. This didn't surprise Mamma, because she had always been able to foretell the future. I would watch her read playing cards for friends and think how clever she was. Her grandmother and her great-grandmother had both been psychic too. But with me, it was flowing like Niagara Falls and I had no way of controlling it. So she did what I guess any good parent would have done and explored countless subjects in the field of spirituality until she had at least some of the answers to my questions. I have to thank her for supporting my unique gifts, because I'm sure it's made me the person I am today. In turn, her career took off like a rocket, and she is now a nationally known clairvoyant and author.

She was shocked when, at twenty-three, I began casting spells for the things I wanted. She, like many others, had always regarded witchcraft as some kind of dark art, and she proceeded to haul me over the coals for dabbling in such things. It was only when I pointed out that Wicca was just a word for everything we already believed in that she took a step back and listened to me. Just as Christians light candles and pray to angels, I also lit candles and prayed to angels. The only difference was that I had a wand in my pocket, potions and herbs on my altar, and a broomstick propping up the hearth! I was doing nothing wrong. I wasn't casting spells to hurt or hinder another human being, nor was I about to zap anyone who got on my nerves. I was simply being the white witch I was always destined to be.

Then one day in the winter of 2003 I had a vision. I would write books and teach courses to reinforce the message that witchcraft is a positive force. After all, this is the twenty-first century—why do so many still carry the belief that witchcraft is evil and ungodly? It was as if someone in the spirit world had tapped me on the shoulder and bellowed in my ear, because I suddenly had this passionate desire to write. Now I'm a bit like a witchy advice columnist who makes it all better with a wave of the wand, offering spells and potions to those with problems.

Just like everyone else who is walking this planet, I am on a journey. Shawn is on her own journey, and somehow our paths crossed and we ventured into writing this book together. It's been a wonderful experience to discover how another witch, nearly 3,500 miles away, practices her craft. Most of our teachings are similar, and of course some are different, but one important thing we have in common is that we also share a desire to strive for the greater good—and we are both having a lot of fun along the way!

USING PRACTICAL MAGICK IN EVERYDAY LIFE

It's electrifying to consider how the power of positive thinking and believing in your inner self can make almost anything possible. Well, it most certainly can, and for those of you who want to access this power, this book will give you information about all aspects of modern-day witchcraft and teach you how to cast spells positively so you get better results.

In the chapters ahead, we will look at how witches today go about their magickal business, offering as well some traditional methods for comparison. Witchcraft today is a little different from the ancient teachings; just like many other things, it has evolved with the times. Nowadays, we can access spell ingredients all year round, whereas the pagan folk in centuries past had only seasonal items to work with. We can hop on the Internet and order herbs and potions from all four corners of the earth. Additionally, the global network has expanded our knowledge and helped us to learn about other cultures and belief systems. With this huge melting pot of options, today's witches are better educated and more sophisticated than our pagan ancestors. We have updated our methods and brought witchcraft into the twenty-first century.

Although there are modern Wiccans who still worship the traditional gods and goddesses, many witches—including Shawn and me—

prefer a newer branch of witchcraft based on angel energy, known as Angelic Wicca.

People who follow the essence of Angelic Wicca respect the earth and all things living. They often have a fascination with growing and tending plants, so you usually find them up to their armpits in a pile of soil. Among modern Wiccans there is also an ever-growing interest in holistic practices such as Reiki, aromatherapy, and reflexology, and today's witch often delights in reading tarot cards or studying topics such as palmistry or astrology. Because most Wiccans have a deep-seated faith in the power of the universe and the Divine Creator, they revel in things supernatural and esoteric and enjoy the mysteries of the unexplained, from runes to UFOs to telepathy.

THE HISTORY

It is a sad fact, but a fact nonetheless, that over many centuries magick has had dark or disturbing connotations. It is only now that society is starting to see that witchcraft is just like any other faith. We can thank books, TV programs, and films such as *Charmed*, *Merlin*, and the Harry Potter series for today's positive interest in all things magickal. Historically, though, in most cases witchcraft was never a sinister practice; it was just some early peoples' way of respectfully utilizing the ingredients of life, provided by the Divine Source, for physical and spiritual healing and protection. Let's delve back a few thousand years to the days of Mr. and Mrs. Pagan. First, because there was no grocery store, Mr. Pagan would venture out with his spear in hand and kill a deer or a rabbit to take home for lunch, or Mrs. Pagan would go out picking berries and fruit from the nearby trees and bushes. Compared to us today, our ancestors worked far more with their natural instincts, a talent we have mostly lost touch with in our high-tech world. As a way of thanking the gods for a good crop, fine weather, and a hearty meal, the Pagans would often sacrifice one or two of their animals in thanks. Today, we would be outraged by this behavior, but back then, they considered it the proper way to honor their gods.

If Mr. Pagan had a pounding headache after hunting all day, a fever, or some even worse malady, he couldn't stop in the local pharmacy to buy a bottle of aspirin. Instead, the men or women of the village (often the women) would scour the hedgerows for herbs and plants that they believed could cure the problem. Over the generations, the herb gatherers learned a lot about the properties of the local flora, and their remedies and concoctions were passed down from parents to children, paving the way for many of the antibiotics and painkilling drugs we use today. Those who were knowledgeable about the healing properties of plants and flowers were often considered to be "medicine men" and "wise women" and were regarded as the doctors and midwives of their time.

Because the pagans were simple people, they automatically interpreted phenomena such as shooting stars or freak storms as signs from the gods. Perhaps they were signs—there are many today who believe that natural disasters and bizarre occurrences are harbingers of things to come. We may have lost our connection with our instinctive wisdom over the centuries, but most people still have a tendency to be superstitious to some degree.

THE DEVIL IS IN THE DETAILS

From the fourteenth to the eighteenth centuries, for complex reasons that scholars are still studying, waves of paranoia, hysteria, and suspicion set off witch hunts throughout the Western world, where those accused of witchcraft and trafficking with the devil were tried in both ecclesiastical and secular courts. It is estimated that sixty thousand people—mostly women—were executed. Sadly, witches have yet to shake off the bad press that has followed them for centuries; even today, witchcraft is typically associated with the horned devil and all things evil. This gets my goat (no pun intended!) because it could not be farther from the truth. It gets tiresome having to explain to misinformed individuals that just because we are happy to call ourselves witches, that does not mean we are devil worshippers or Satanists. In fact, we are quite the opposite.

Witches believe that the Creator has given us life to improve our souls and cultivate our wisdom. Lesser mortals, and some religious faiths, blame an evil entity such as the devil for the negativity that mankind creates. But witches do not believe in the devil, because the devil does not exist in our eyes. Are there despicable people in the world? Yes, definitely. Do these people become evil entities when they die? Probably. But a good thing to remember is that in each and every person's DNA there is a spark of the Creator, and with this Divine Power we can go forth to improve our imperfections.

WICCAN WAY OF LIFE

Contrary to popular belief, witches are not just female; they can be male too. It is perfectly okay if a guy wants to be referred to as a witch—the term can be applied to either gender—but more often than not, he will use the term *wizard*, the masculine equivalent.

We witches have evolved with the times: we no longer walk around in pointy hats and flowing gowns, and these days we ride vacuum cleaners instead of broomsticks. Joking aside, the foundation of our faith is much the same as it was hundreds of years ago. Witches believe that we are not born alone, nor do we die alone, and that once we enter this world we are accompanied by one or two spirit helpers who have been assigned to us by a higher source. We refer to these helpers as our guides and angels. We believe that nothing in this life is a coincidence, so we are always on the lookout for signs from them.

Wicca is an open-minded faith that you can fine-tune to suit your own needs. There is no specific rule book to follow, so it doesn't matter if you want to practice lightly and cast the odd spell here and there or immerse yourself completely. I like to describe Wicca as a way of life rather than a religion, so if parts of it don't ring true to your soul, you can simply eliminate those parts and find approaches you are more comfortable with. With Angelic Wicca, there is no right or wrong way, just as long as you keep in mind that witches work for the good of humankind and never set out to harm others. When you have learned what you need to know, you can then strive to gain more control over the day-to-day issues that crop up in your life and also go on to discover the importance of your life force and the significance of your faith.

Generally speaking, there are two types of witches. First, there is the eccentric witch who is a tad unconventional and waltzes around in long, flowing skirts and plays with imaginary unicorns in the backyard. Shocked? Well, don't be. These Wiccans are in fact very sweet and not the slightest bit nutty; they are just very much in tune with their creative sides, and if they can see fairies in the kitchen cupboards, who are we to argue? Then there's the other type, like Shawn and me. We are straightforward, feet-on-the-ground witches who are caught between having a great sense of spiritual understanding and being very levelheaded at the same time.

That's why Wicca rings true to me—because at the end of the day, it's an uncomplicated faith. Witches welcome and worship the simple things in life. Most of the things we believe in are actually tangible, not wrapped up in myths, legends, or fairy tales. For me, it's easy to understand the importance of the moon, because it's right up there in the sky and it has a powerful effect on the rhythms of Earth. Wiccans recognize and appreciate the significance of our planet in the same way. When you take a good, close look at nature, it is pretty remarkable how most things are in perfect balance. Next time you sit quietly in the garden or enjoy a tranquil walk in a field, just stop for a second and take in the wonder of it all. You will notice the birds singing their own songs, the ants busily working as a team, and, on frosty mornings, the delicate spiderwebs hanging like lace on the hedges. We believe that everything has a spirit, everything has a soul, and that most things happen for a reason.

COVENS

Sometimes practicing Wicca can be a lonely pursuit, because there may not be that many like-minded people in your circle of friends. This is why some witches like to join a coven: a group of Wiccan followers who share their spells and rituals and unite once a month to perform their magick communally, using their collective energy to give the spells more power. The word *coven* often brings to mind a scene of thirteen or so haggish, wart-ridden women dancing naked around a campfire. In truth, today's meetings often consist of a few witches (a minimum of three) hanging out, usually on a full moon, drinking a glass or two of something pleasant, and talking amicably about various things, including their recent experiences with spell casting and other magickal matters. They'll be dressed in jeans and T-shirts and not the long black flowing gowns that fairy tales depict.

Today, there are online covens with chat rooms and forums so that witches from all over the world can get together and communicate freely. Some of these sites have as many as three hundred witches registered as members. This is lovely, because not only does it allow us to coordinate our spell casting so that we can all cast together at the same time, it also lets us learn about the different Wiccan cultures around the world. Online covens are often more practical, too, because local gatherings tend to go underground for fear of being publicly ridiculed. Hopefully, in the near future this will become unnecessary as people accept witchcraft more and more for the faith it is, not as so many history books have negatively depicted it.

Throughout this book, you will get a better understanding of our practices and principles, and as you read on, you may be able to identify some of our beliefs with your own. Wicca is not a prescribed religion, it is simply a way of life. Who knows, you may already be living as witches without even realizing it!

A WITCH'S TOOL KIT

There are some implements witches simply cannot live without and quite a few more they may just like to have. Some of you may want to follow tradition and accumulate several of the ancient tools to make your "tool kit" as authentic as possible. However, this isn't always necessary. Your spells and rituals will still work even if you use the bare basics. Modern witches such as Shawn tend to toss aside a lot of the old apparatus and incorporate some modern appliances into their spell casting, whereas I like the idea of creating a timeless atmosphere with my spells, so I use vintage tools if I can get my hands on them. Whatever assemblage you decide on, it is key that you feel comfortable with the tools you choose.

The required tools vary from spell to spell. There are a few rituals that don't require any implements at all, but for most, a selection of candles and herbs is generally kept close at hand, as well as tools such as the pentagram (to represent the five elements), crystals (to energize the area), and salt (to sanctify the space).

Many people are discouraged from casting certain spells because the ingredients or tools are hard to get hold of, but you can be as flexible as you want, and it is okay to improvise. There are, however, several items you'll certainly need.

ESSENTIAL TOOLS

THE ALTAR

A base to work on, called an altar, is highly recommended. You should create your own altar and personalize it to your taste with whatever charms and objects speak to you.

Some homes do not have space to accommodate a full-size altar, which can be anything from a large coffee table to a dining table. If space is an issue, you can use a shelf, tabletop, small coffee table, or mantelpiece. Some witches born under a fire or earth sign prefer to cast their spells directly on natural wood, while others like covering their altars in cloth, which can be bought inexpensively at fabric shops. If you do opt for a cloth, the best color to use is lavender or deep purple. In Wiccan circles, the color purple is thought to be the most positive color to attract spiritual fulfillment. It is also associated with chakra balancing and healing and will create the perfect mood for your magick.

If you have already come "out of the closet" as a witch to your friends and family, you can leave your altar set up in a main area all the time so that when you need to conduct a ritual, you can access it quickly. Witches who want to be more discreet can create a portable altar by placing a cloth on the floor and laying out the tools on top. This method is also handy if you are traveling and want to take your altar with you.

THE PENTACLE

One of the most essential items a witch uses when casting spells is the symbol of a five-pointed star, known as a pentacle or pentagram. Believed to date back more than five thousand years to ancient Mesopotamia, the pentagram has been a powerful and positive symbol for many different religions throughout history, as well as in alchemy. In pagan times the symbol was often worn as an amulet for spiritual protection and to ensure a safe, happy homecoming. The five points of the star represent the five elements; spirit is the topmost point, and the other points, moving in a clockwise direction, are water, fire, earth, and air.

When turned upside down, the pentacle assumes the shape of a goat, symbolizing the horned god of some neo-pagan faiths. At some point in Western history—the actual date is debated by scholars—the five-pointed star became erroneously equated with Satan and devil worship. As time went on, those working on the darker side of magick adopted the down-turned pentagram sign that often appears in horror movies

today. Because of the bad press, and probably because most witches want
to practice purely white magick and not associate themselves with anything
negative, we tend to use the pentacle in the more familiar upright position that,
if you look closely, resembles the form of a human: the top point of the star is
the head, the outer points represent the arms, and the lower points correspond
to the legs. Many witches wear pentagram necklaces and earrings as a form of
protection or as a way for fellow witches to recognize them.

When casting spells, it is always best to have this symbol on your person
or somewhere on your altar. You can either draw a simple pentagram or, if
you are an artistic soul, create a more ornate centerpiece with painted glass or
something similar. As you set up your altar, place the pentacle directly in the
center so that you can arrange the other items all around it. The size of the five-
pointed star doesn't matter in the slightest. You can have a full-size dinner-plate
version or just a small earring.

Whatever kind of pentagram you choose to use, you should first "charge"
it. This is a straightforward procedure that will cleanse and bless the pentagram
and imbue it with magickal energy. The best way to do this is to leave your
pentagram outside overnight in your garden or on your front porch or window
ledge during a full moon phase; this approach charges the pentagram naturally.
You can also charge other tools, such as crystals and talismans, this way to give
them extra potency. Once the pentagram is charged and placed in the center of
the altar, it will ward off negativity and act as your source of protection.

CANDLES

Candles represent the elements fire and air. Most spells will include a
candle or two, or even more, so always have a selection of different colors
at hand. Traditionally, you start with one main white candle on the altar

to neutralize the energies. This is usually centered toward the back of the altar. There is no need to inscribe or anoint this candle, but blessing it with water is a good idea. To do this, dip your fingers in some bottled water and run them over the candle while saying, "This candle is now cleansed and blessed." Dry the candle with paper towels. For more information on inscribing and anointing candles, candle colors, and candle spells, see chapter 5.

INCENSE

Burning incense while a spell is in progress is an absolute must. Its magickal properties help create the perfect atmosphere and boost any spell's potency. However, there are so many varieties to choose from that it can be difficult to determine which ones to use. I have seven types in my tool kit that cover almost any situation. If you have trouble finding the right one for your spell, simply burn sage to cleanse your work space.

BASIL: An aromatic scent that is used for attracting wealth and prosperity and in fertility rituals.

EUCALYPTUS: Centers and balances emotions; excellent for helping make decisions.

FRANKINCENSE: A wonderful spiritual disinfectant. Burn this if anyone in the family has a bad cold, or use generally with any health spells. If you are trying to ward off coughs and colds, it might be a good idea to burn this in a different room from where the patient is sitting, to avoid irritation from the smoke.

OPIUM: Induces sleep and invigorates your psychic senses. If you are an insomniac, light an incense stick about an hour before bed and you'll sleep like a baby.

SAGE: Used as a smudging stick or burned as incense, this will cleanse your space in preparation for a spell. Its magick automatically dispels any negative energy, leaving the space free from bad vibes.

SANDALWOOD: A warm, gentle, woody fragrance to relax you and ease distress.

YLANG-YLANG: A sweet and heady perfume that enhances any love spell. Use for attracting new love, harmonizing marriages, and healing impotency problems.

SOIL AND WATER

These substances symbolize the natural elements of earth and water and bring balance and harmony to your work space. A small bowl or an eggcup of garden soil should sit to one side of the pentagram, and the water—in a similar vessel—should sit on the other side (see "Chalice," page 14).

SALT

Salt is a fantastic source of protection and is used in many spells to banish anything evil. Either sprinkle a little sea salt over your altar cloth or put some on the altar in a small bowl.

OPTIONAL TOOLS

CHALICE

The chalice symbolizes fertility; in times past, its bowl represented the womb of the Goddess. The base of the vessel signified our world as we know it and the stem suggested human rapport with the spirits. I have a chalice on my altar that holds magickal water, but whenever I cast spells to help someone get pregnant, I empty out the chalice and fill it with fresh basil leaves instead.

CAULDRON

This magickal vessel is probably the most recognizable symbol of witchcraft after the broomstick. Today, the cauldron can be used as a vessel for making infusions and potions (although a microwave can be used for many such spells; see chapter 6). For spells that involve burning herbs, the cauldron, typically fashioned from copper or cast iron, is still a useful object. Lots of witches like to have cauldrons on display in their houses and also use them to store their herbs. Cauldrons used to be difficult to find, but now they are available online. I have spent many years collecting cauldrons and have a large selection. When I moved to my farm some seven years ago, I got out my faithful metal detector and dug an old cast-iron one out of the ground. Maybe I am not the only witch who has ever resided here!

BELL

Used primarily in banishment spells, a bell can be rung to indicate that a spell is about to begin or tinkled repeatedly around the home to get rid of unwanted vibrations. I always walk around the house ringing my bell when the kids have been bickering or anyone has been upset. It sounds bizarre, but it really does settle down a bad atmosphere and leave a place feeling calm again.

ATHAME

An athame is a ceremonial knife, typically black-handled with a double-edged blade; it is an ancient tool that you don't see on many witches' altars today. Some witches inscribe their candles with the athame or use it to cast a magickal circle around the altar before commencing a spell. To cast a magickal circle, hold the knife in your right hand and draw a circle clockwise over the altar, a few inches above the items on it. An athame works by conducting your power through it, and it is to be used only for magickal purposes—not for gutting fish or peeling potatoes! Like cauldrons, athames are now easy to purchase online.

WAND

A witch wouldn't be a witch without a wand, and I have to say, I do love mine. By tradition, wands are usually crafted from the wood of the willow, elder, apple, or cherry tree.

Today you can easily buy a wand online or in a specialty store, but the real magick in a wand is channeled into it by its maker, so, if possible, try making your own. If you decide to get creative and make a wand yourself, you can craft it from any tree branch that you feel an affinity for, and you should always thank the tree for sharing its wood with you.

Wands come in many shapes and sizes; the width is not that important, but the length of the wand should measure from your elbow to the tip of your index finger. You can carve designs into the wood or smooth it down with sandpaper before finally varnishing it and then charging it in the same way you would a pentagram. Make your wand as ornate or as rustic as you like. I carefully decorated mine with gold paint and glued a big chunk of quartz crystal to the tip of it.

For spell-casting purposes, the wand is used as a summoning tool and also to bless and charge objects.

Before a ritual begins, you can touch each object on your altar with the end of your wand to transfer its natural earthly energy to the items and add a little extra magick. Some witches like to "draw down the moon" prior to casting a spell. This is a very old tradition that involves standing outside during a full moon phase and pointing the wand at the moon. It is thought that the moon's power charges the wand, making its magick more powerful.

BROOMSTICK

In witchy circles, the round-bottom broomstick, or besom, as it is more commonly known, is actually a fertility symbol, long used by female witches in fertility rites and to sweep away negativity. The sweep, or brush, corresponds to the female genitalia, and the staff is associated with the male phallus—therefore it is a symbol of the male and the female combined.

Often a besom was propped up near the hearth of a witch's home to keep evil energy from entering through the chimney. Some modern witches still follow this practice, but many just display the besom as a Wiccan home decoration and embellish it with pretty flowers and dried herbs. Of course, besoms always were and still are popular at handfastings (Wiccan weddings; see chapter 11), where couples jump over the broom to display their union.

CRYSTALS AND GEMSTONES

Crystals possess a pure, natural magick. I always keep at least three on my altar. See chapter 8 to read more about crystals and learn which ones will best spruce up your spell.

FEATHERS

Because most of our spells invoke angelic energy, placing a selection of feathers on the altar will entice our angels to visit us. You can color-coordinate the feathers with the candles you are using in a particular ritual or simply use white for purity and peace.

THE BOOK OF SHADOWS

A Book of Shadows is a kind of journal or diary that witches keep close at hand for jotting down and recording their spells. You can use any type of notebook for your Book of Shadows, but because it is a treasury, many witches prefer to use a nice leather-bound book or something a little fancier. When you cast a spell, write down in the book all the details of the ritual, such as the date, the ingredients you used, and the phase of the moon. Leave a space underneath to record the results. Many ancient spells have been passed down through the centuries in this way, and, at last count, I think I had seventeen of these books—you could say I have a bit of a witchy library. If you would rather record your spells on the computer, you can create a folder on your desktop for your Book of Shadows, but please remember to back it up because computers have a habit of crashing and, once lost, your findings will be gone forever!

PART ONE

THE SPIRITUAL WORLD

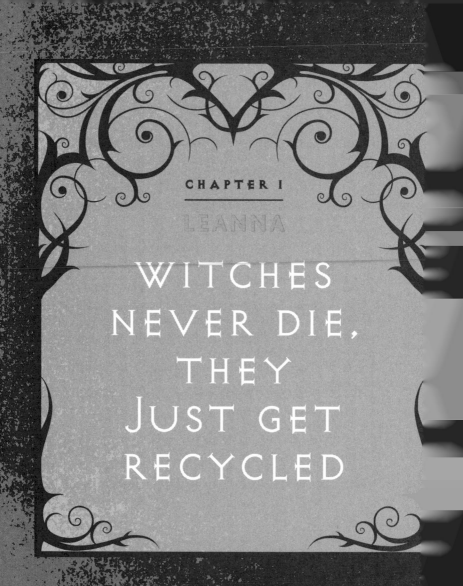

CHAPTER I

LEANNA

WITCHES
NEVER DIE,
THEY
JUST GET
RECYCLED

WHAT IS THIS LIFE ABOUT AND why are we here? Is there an afterlife? I get asked these questions a lot, especially by teenage witches who are curious to know the purpose of life and death. I usually answer by saying that a belief in an afterlife is a personal thing to each and every one of us, so you need to explore as many options as possible and then listen to your soul to find the truth for yourself.

Most witches throughout the world have a deep belief in reincarnation and the afterlife. Common sense tells us that living a life span of approximately eighty years and then just disappearing forever would be pointless. What could we possibly learn from that? Nothing—and so the modern-day witch tends to think along the same lines as many other religions and faiths, taking comfort in believing that our spirit lives on after we die.

Imagine that your body is an automobile and it transports your spirit around for the duration of your life. Just like an automobile, your body occasionally breaks down and needs repairing. A little tune-up every now and again will keep it in peak performing condition, and of course, you'll need to put the right gas in the engine in the form of healthy food. But no matter how good a caretaker you are, the body that is your vehicle can't possibly last forever. Once it takes its last drive, your soul steps right out of it and, after a little rest with your loved ones in spirit, gets back into another vehicle. This is the crux of reincarnation: your soul gets a new car to drive around the Earth in again, so to speak.

WHAT IS THE PURPOSE OF REINCARNATION?

Some people really don't understand reincarnation; they wonder why we would want to keep coming back over and over again. It's a bit idealistic to think that we can have just one life and then retire to a fluffy pink cloud for the rest of eternity! You may well get to the ultimate resting place someday, but before you do, you have some work to do.

There are three reasons for reincarnating:

* To work on overcoming your faults
* To experience every human emotion possible
* To eventually become a part of the Divine Power

When a soul is born, it begins a journey of spiritual development. With every incarnation on Earth, we learn valuable lessons that help us on the journey and go on to make us the true individuals we are. It's a bit like being in school. Sometimes the lessons we face are painless and we can sail through them with ease. At other times, they can be hard-hitting and difficult, making us face arduous challenges head-on.

Take, for example, a person who seems to experience trials and tribulations on a constant basis. From a spiritual perspective, what is this all about? Once you have undergone a lesson and have learned it properly, you won't have to go through it again. That chapter of your life will be over and you will move on to other lessons. You might think that it's unfair to have to go through problematic situations, especially if others around you seem to have it easier, but each lesson we face gives us an internal strength that can never be taken away from us. Call it character-building. These lessons enhance our inner wisdom, which is what we are all ultimately striving for. This is how it goes, life after life, until you've learned all you need to know.

I once knew someone who was very placid, and whatever job he went into, he was faced with a heavy-handed boss. He would get terribly upset and move from one company to another in a bid to avoid these difficult people; but with each new job, he was cursed with another grueling manager. I pointed out to him that maybe his lesson was to toughen up and not play the wounded victim all the time. I advised him to change his approach and stand up for what he thought was right. He took my advice, and shortly afterward, the oppressing supervisor was dismissed from his job for harassing other members of the staff! Since then, then my friend has gained confidence in dealing with overpowering people, and he has not had to face a situation like that again.

REINCARNATION RELAXES THE SOUL

We are all reincarnating at different rates. This is why some people are truly wonderful and some are, well, not. Those who seem incredibly sensitive and loving are probably way ahead of the prickly, spiteful people in the reincarnation process.

When you meet lovely, kind, and caring people, it is probable that they have reincarnated many times. Their endless incarnations have raised their spirits' vibration, so they automatically show patience and strive to do everything right in their lives. People who are mean, selfish, and egotistic probably haven't reincarnated as much. That isn't to say that these people are wicked; they simply haven't learned all their lessons yet. Think of them as bratty adolescents and the sympathetic ones as the grandparents of the reincarnation process—regardless of their age!

DEALING WITH THE DARK SIDE

It's safe to say that every person walking this planet is imperfect—if we were all without flaws, there would be no point in even being here—but some people's souls are darker than others. Our world is home to many such young, disruptive souls. These people may physically or emotionally hurt others, bully the more sensitive or vulnerable among us, and generally cause mayhem. This is probably because the young soul hasn't yet developed the wisdom or empathy for others that it should and because it has chosen to follow a bad path. We all have a choice—to follow a good path or a bad one. I don't mean to say that we all started out as murderers and rapists at the beginning of our reincarnation process, though; we are all individuals with free will. We all climb the spiritual ladder at our own pace.

After a lifetime of doing harm, this type of soul is counseled on the other side by the elders (guides and angels), who try to help the soul see the error of its ways. Sometimes counseling doesn't help, and so the soul, when it reincarnates, is born into a situation where it will learn the lesson firsthand; this is where the law of karma comes into play. And sometimes those who failed to be upright and honorable while they were alive carry these same soul traits into the afterlife, but decide to remain in a dark astral realm and not reincarnate. This means that bad spirits really do exist, and it's important to protect yourself from them.

Many Wiccans, whether working in a solitary way or in a coven, will make a point, once or twice a year, of uniting with fellow witches to perform ritualistic candle spells. At this time, they all band together and ask the angels for a higher consciousness for those who are considered evil. We believe that prayer and ritual are all-powerful and can shift the negative energies around malevolent people and spirits, leaving more positive energy behind. Later in the book we will learn about such spells, and we'll also take a look at magickal methods of protection. Rest assured, you will find out how to keep a safe distance from these spooky spirits.

WHAT COMES AROUND

If you tread on the heads of a few people on the way up, you may just meet them on the way down! It's safe to say that whatever weakness or shortfall there is in your personality, your life will expose it in some way. Until you resolve the problem, you will keep reincarnating.

You may be graced with a life of wealth and power, enabling you to shoot right up the corporate ladder and deck yourself out in diamond tiaras. Just because you have the crown jewels on your head doesn't mean that you are better than others; in fact, you are being tested by the spirit world to see exactly what you are going to do with all your good fortune.

If you don't put that money energy to good use, but turn into a mean old miser, keeping it all for yourself, the next time around you may be plunged into a life of poverty. Having an experience like this teaches the soul a very important lesson: however much you desire those diamond tiaras, you just can't afford them, and so, hopefully, you will begin to appreciate what matters most—your friends, your family, being together, being compassionate. Sharing the little pleasures may begin to seem much more significant.

I always admire celebrities and business-people who give a lot of their fortune to charity, especially if they came from poor backgrounds themselves. Regardless of how much money they have, their feet are still firmly on the ground. These souls probably lived impoverished lives at some stage, and now, with many reincarnations under their belts, they are quite happy to spread their good fortune around. This automatically scores them good karma points for the future.

SMALL STEPS ON A LONG JOURNEY

We can't truly empathize with others until we have actually experienced their situation firsthand. The theory of reincarnation gives us that opportunity, even if we don't always recognize it for what it is. Have you ever turned on the news and gotten upset about what you see, be it a local disaster or a large-scale catastrophe? Has your heart cried out and left you carrying a distraught feeling around all day? These emotions could stem from a memory of a previous life. Perhaps you underwent something similar and the situation has reawakened something in your subconscious.

Often, a person doesn't need a series of lives to try and help others who have suffered a comparable fate. You find many battered wives opening shelters for those who are going through violent relationships, abused children going on to be social workers, and former drug addicts becoming substance-abuse counselors. You can see the lessons here. These people are using their experiences as a way of helping others to deal with similar emotional issues in the space of one lifetime. Spiritually, this is highly commendable and another step up the ladder.

FRIENDS SENT TO LEAD US HOME

A witch firmly believes that everything we do with our lives is examined when we return *home*, or to the spirit world. Every good deed we perform and every bad thing we do and feel is scrutinized. However, this scrutiny isn't Judgment Day for witches. Our actions are closely observed by our spirit helpers because our main aim is to improve ourselves and they want to assist us in being the best we can be. If we behave inappropriately or make serious mistakes in a life, we are not hauled over the coals by our spirit guides when we go home. They know that we sometimes fall off the spiritual wagon. They have unconditional love for us, and they are very patient and understanding. Their job is to plod along with us until we get it right.

Guides, or "white lighters," as they are often called today, are souls who have more or less completed their reincarnations. They have lived endless lives, learned countless lessons, and gone on to "graduate." I must stress, though, that guides are not perfect by any means. They still have the odd flaw here and there, and they are working with us to raise their vibration even further (kind of like charity work on the spiritual level). Contrary to the belief that we are born alone and we die alone, we are not actually expected to reincarnate all by ourselves. Each and every one of us has at least one guide who acts as our escort and mentor and often speaks to our subconscious when we are sleeping. Have you ever gone to bed at night really angry with someone, only to wake up the next morning and find that all those feelings have disappeared? Your guide may have come to you while you were sleeping and helped you sort out your issues with the other person. Guides can also come to us when we meditate or act as our muses when we need inspiration. They assist us in times of crisis and are invaluable to our spiritual development.

When I was ten years old, I actually saw my guide. All my young life, I had suffered with dreadful ear infections, and this was one of those distressing times. During the night, I dreamed that a young blond boy sat down on my bed and placed his hands over my ears. I asked him what his name was and he replied, "Erik." I asked him what he was doing and he said he was going to heal me. In the dream, I was aware of being totally safe and secure; I felt as if I'd touched hands with an old friend. The next morning my ear infection had completely vanished, so much so that I could discontinue the medicine I was taking. It was like I had never had an infection at all!

Over the years I have seen Erik many times in dream sleep, especially when something significant is going to happen to me. Nowadays, though, he is around my age, so, in a way, I guess he's grown up with me. I've since learned that children's guides often take on the physical appearance of a child to make their charges feel more comfortable. This could give a whole new meaning to the term "imaginary friends," don't you think?

LEARN YOUR LESSONS WELL

While life is a series of tests, no one gives you a report card upon your death. Your reactions to situations are watched very closely in the spirit world, but you won't be chastised if you slip up a few times. Witches know that before we finish reincarnating, we need to experience every single human emotion, so it's safe to say that by the time we reach a state of perfection, each of us could have lived a thousand times!

From here on in, try to do at least one nice thing for another person every day. Smile at the postman, check in on that elderly neighbor, or take a few minutes out of your busy day to ask how someone is doing. Once you get into the habit of being pleasant to others, it will become second nature, and your vibration will be buzzing with positive energy.

Shawn's Tip

Be kind to others. Help when and where you can. Don't judge. Be thankful for what you have. And look forward to reaching that highest level of reincarnation—it may be bumpy sometimes, but it's going to be a heck of a ride!

CHAPTER 2

LEANNA

ANGELS

ANGEL MANIA IS SPREADING ACROSS THE world, and angels are becoming more and more popular as each year passes. These beautiful beings have always had their place in the craft, but they used to play a secondary role to the more traditional Wiccan gods and goddesses. Today, you won't find many British witches connecting with the gods and goddesses, though there are branches of Wicca in the United States and elsewhere that do. On a relatively new path called Angelic Wicca, which my mother, Beleta Greenaway, and I informally helped to develop several decades ago in England, most spells and rituals are directed to the angelic energies instead. This is no slur on our ancient teachings; just as most things evolve with the times, so has witchcraft. There are still some witches who prefer the conventional gods and goddesses, and it's perfectly okay to work with them if that's what your heart is telling you. You can adapt all the spells in this book to summon your god or goddess for your needs, whatever they may be.

Angels reside in a different realm from ours, one that is ideal in every way. In traditional religions they are portrayed as pure, beautiful, shining winged creatures living alongside God as heavenly assistants, divine messengers, and guides and guardians to humans.

Angels have long played and still do play an important part in many faiths, but, as with many supernatural beings, no one can say with certainty what they are like. Lots of people profess to have seen one of these beautiful beings firsthand, but sadly, I have not had the pleasure. While I like to think that there are male and female angels out there, some people believe them to be androgynous. I've studied many books over the years on angels; some state that they are genderless, while others depict them as having a gender. I personally go with my heart on this one. In a way, it makes it easier for me to relate to angels if I see them as men or women, especially when I call on them so often.

In my research, I have found that not only do they have an inner beauty, angels are commonly thought to be quite glamorous in appearance too. Those who have been fortunate enough to see angels often remark on their radiant colors, heavenly smiles, and never-ending patience. Children have more encounters with angels than adults, on average; because children haven't been on the planet very long, they are much closer to the spirit world than we are and can more easily tap into their psychic portals.

ANGEL ON YOUR SHOULDER

Angels are said to be able to take any form and adapt to the needs and beliefs of the humans they are trying to help. The angel's aim is not to frighten. For instance, a child might be frightened to see a huge winged spirit sitting at the foot of the bed, so an angel appearing to a child might morph into something

a little less dramatic, such as a dot of dancing light or a spirit child. This allows the child to interact with the angel and get used to its vibration. The angel then grows in size and maturity as the child grows and matures.

When I was a child, I often saw the spirit of a beautiful blond dog that would appear for a few seconds every now and again. I instinctively knew that it was a positive presence and there to protect me. The lucky few who have seen a winged angel in person remark that angel wings are not like birds' wings, but actually glowing lights that oscillate from the angels' "bodies." This light creates streams of healing energy that vibrate with shimmering hues—colors that are difficult to describe because they are not seen in this world.

When I was about six years old, I was very inquisitive about angels and always fired probing questions at my poor mother. One day, I innocently asked her if angels had sex. She choked on her coffee before composing herself, then went on to reassure me that angels were far too pure and godly to resort to such primitive acts. Of course, me being me, I had an answer for everything, and I retorted that she obviously had it wrong, because there were lots and lots of baby cherubs out there! I believe her reply was: "Cherubs have been created, Dear, as baby angels, and remain as cherubs for human children to play with." What a nice thought!

EARTH ANGELS

Many people do not realize that angels can also take on human form and materialize as ordinary folk. An angel could be the person you meet in passing when you are taking a stroll on the beach, or the passenger sitting next to you on the bus chattering about something or nothing. Sometimes they appear just to see how you are doing, sometimes to lend a hand and pick you up if you fall flat on your face.

Angels have also been known to magickally intervene when something is destined or not destined to happen. Have you ever wondered at the coincidences in your life or marveled at times when you came out of dangerous situations unscathed? There is a great deal of angelic intervention going on in the world, and there are angels interacting with us all the time.

Just as we all have our own spirit guides (which are different from angels), each and every one of us has an angel watching over us too. If you are in the wrong place at the wrong time, be assured that your guardian angel will be there. Although sometimes you need to directly experience a harmful situation because it's a lesson you have to undergo, your guardian angel will be present to guide you if it's your fate to come out unscathed. There are countless stories about people being saved from disaster at the last moment; I'm sure you've heard or experienced a few yourself, and there are many books that go into this in detail to convince us that we are not alone. In 2009, my mother wrote *Simply Angels*, which has a wealth of information on all aspects of angelic vibrations. Here, we'll answer just a few of the more common questions about angels.

HOW MANY ARE OUT THERE?

How many angels are in the universe? There are millions, trillions, and zillions of angels on the spirit plane, each with their own particular talents. There are angels for healing, love, money, animals, children . . . the list is endless. Just as life evolves, angels have too, and every situation you can imagine has an angel representing it. Whatever your problem, there is an angel to assist you, and if you simply ask one for help, you will be shielded and guided throughout your time of uncertainty.

If we work toward becoming perfect in our lifetimes and manage to get off the reincarnating wheel one day, we can go and be with the angels. Just for the record, I think it will be a while before I get to go join them, because I tend to laugh at saucy jokes, drink far too much red wine, and on occasion lust after Richard Gere. But with all that said, I am sure that angels have the most amazing sense of humor and, because they strive to promote happiness and laughter, often have a giggle at our expense.

WHAT HAPPENS WHEN YOU SUMMON AN ANGEL?

Wicca is ideal for summoning angels. They like you to make an effort and set up a pretty table or altar with lots of decorative objects in place. Crystals set the right ambience, as do incense, flowers, pictures, and, most important, candles. Before you start, ring a little bell over the altar to get rid of any negative vibrations. Try not to leave any junk lying around, as it is believed that angels love cleanliness and purity—although they will still guide and shield you even if the laundry is not folded and put away. They are also partial to lovely smells and aromas, so make sure you have some essential oils around. You can play peaceful music, but it might be a good idea to put the cat out of the room, if you have one, as cats home in on celestial vibrations like bees to a flower and can bring your beautifully arranged altar crashing to the ground. On one occasion,

Oliver, my Siamese assassin, leaped onto my angelic table, stuck his claws into my gorgeous purple tablecloth, and heaved the entire contents onto the floor.

When invoking an angel, always speak out loud, in your clearest and most earnest voice. You don't have to speak in Old English or use any religious wording; your everyday language is fine. You might ask if the angel could do you a favor or help you with something, or simply ask them to listen. Try to look at the angel as your best friend or confidant.

How Do I Know I Am Summoning the Right Angel?

It's not that difficult. A thought or a prayer is a powerful thing, so whatever you send out mentally or verbally, the right angel will usually receive it and respond. Each angel does have a name, but it's really not necessary to know all the different names; they will decide among themselves who is best to support you.

A SIMPLE SPELL TO SUMMON YOUR ANGEL OR GUIDE

Take a few white feathers and scatter them on your altar. Next, place five purple or lavender candles on the table or work surface and arrange them in a circle. Light the candles and visualize yourself surrounded by a purple light. Focus intently on your problem for at least five minutes.

Now recite these words:

Angels of love and beauty, I call upon you this day to help ease my burden. With your inspiring power and influence, show me the solutions I seek.

Then, in your own words (or in a poem you've devised, if you like), go on to describe the kind of help you want. Try to leave nothing out. Remember, the angels can only help us with our dilemmas if we ask them for their help. They are morally bound not to act on our behalf without our asking, because that would be taking away our free will. Close the spell by saying:

So mote it be.

Let the flames burn for an hour and then blow them out. Although this spell is simple—you don't need any tools or ingredients other than the candles and the feathers—it is very dynamic if performed correctly, and within a few short days your problem will diminish and things will start to improve. If you want to make extra sure that the angels are listening, you can repeat this spell and relight the candles the next day.

WHAT DO I TELL THE KIDS?

Children are naturally curious, and if you are practicing Angelic Wicca they will probably take an interest in it too. Let them have a little altar of their own; it will teach them to be creative. They might like to draw a picture of themselves and their angels. If you visit the beach, encourage them to gather shells or pretty driftwood to adorn their space. It's not necessary for them to light candles; I am not an advocate of children playing with matches or lighters under any circumstances.

A child's prayer holds a power all its own, and the angels respond immediately. If your child has a problem of any kind, encourage them to stand over their altar, close their eyes, and tell the angels all about it in their own words. They may not have any problems at all, but just want to ask the angels to help other children who are suffering in the world. It's a nice way to introduce little children to the angelic forces.

My eldest child was four or five when our beloved cat, Nino, went missing for two weeks. Being the cat-mad family we are, we were all frantic with worry, and my son was no exception. He cried himself to sleep for the duration and refused to eat. In a desperate attempt to make him feel better, I helped him set up a little altar, and on it we placed all of Nino's toys, his old collar, and some flower petals from the garden. Hearing a little boy beg the angels to bring back his pet cat has stayed with me for all these years. I am delighted to say that his prayers were answered: that very same night, Nino strolled in the back door, a little the worse for wear, but safe and sound and home at last.

If more than one member of the family is practicing Wicca, you may think it is okay to share your altar and tools, but this is not advisable (which is why I suggested a separate altar for your child). Your personal tools absorb your vibrations and energies, so if you start mixing and matching, the vibes will get confused.

GUARDIAN ANGELS

As witches, the first thing we learn is "protect yourself." Because angels are all-powerful, who better to call upon for protection? I have a little twinkly angel ornament hanging from the rearview mirror in my car, just to give me extra protection when I'm driving (if you put one in your car, just make sure the ornament is small enough not to block your view or distract you while driving—otherwise it might be best to just keep it in your dashboard tray). Any angelic symbol can help to invoke angels, so brooches, jewelry, and knickknacks that you might collect along the way are great for giving you that added safety net. Look at them as lucky angelic charms or amulets.

Angelic Wicca, although not a prescribed religion, teaches us that there are many different types of angels out there. There's one for every human problem and for every human emotion, and once you get the knack of tapping into the energy of angels, you will find that many day-to-day struggles can be resolved this way simply and with ease. For every obstacle in life there is an answer, and with angels' divine intervention we can come to understand more and more about our purpose on this planet. Although I have touched hands with my spirit guide, Erik, my one regret is that I have not been fortunate enough to see these wonderful angelic beings for myself, but who knows—one day I might get lucky!

Shawn's Tip

Each morning, sit quietly for a few minutes and bring an angel into your heart. Ask it to look after you, and repeat this every day so it becomes part of your daily routine. Once you do, it will become like second nature to you. Always be spiritually prepared.

Chapter 3

SHAWN

OUIJA BOARD

MOST PEOPLE HAVE SEEN A OUIJA, OR talking board, at some point in their lives, be it in real life or on a TV show. Although here in the United States most witches gladly accept it as part of the craft, in some countries it is still shied away from. In reality, the Ouija does open up communications between this world and the next. For experienced psychics who know how to use the board properly, it is actually a beneficial tool that can bridge portals into the next world and allow people to communicate with loved ones who have passed over.

WAGNER WIELDS A LITTLE WEIRDNESS

Although various forms of the Ouija board have been used for centuries, Adolphus Theodore Wagner patented the first "talking board"—he called it a psychograph—in England on

January 23, 1854. Rumor has it that Wagner roamed cemeteries in the dark of night, carrying his little wooden board and trying to conjure up the ghosts of dead people. There were also those who whispered under their breath that he was a man possessed, that he walked the streets of London cursing at unseen beings. No one is alive today who knew the man personally, so we may never know what is fact and what is speculation, but since the talking board was closely associated with these stories, it's understandable that people were somewhat reluctant to use it.

However, in the late 1800s, when séances were at the height of their popularity in both Europe and the United States, the talking board was suddenly *en vogue*. People would sit around a table with a medium to guide them in this gentle art of contacting the dead. On the table sat a rectangular playing board with the letters of the alphabet in two curved rows and, underneath the letters, a series of numbers from one through zero. At the top left of the board was the word YES, and at the top right, the word NO.

On the board rested a planchette, a heart-shaped device with three legs that allowed it to glide smoothly across the board.

The medium would ask everyone to rest their fingertips on the planchette, and when the room was quiet enough to hear a pin drop, she would ask the universe if there was anyone present from the "other side" who would like to communicate with those seated at the table. Most people wanted to talk to a loved one who had passed, while others just wanted to know if there was a spirit nearby. The planchette worked by moving around the board and pointing to letters to spell out words in answer to the questions posed.

Leanna's Tip

In Britain we take the Ouija board very seriously, and most white witches use them only rarely. Often, mediums will bring one along to a haunting to establish why a spirit is occupying an area; in cases like these, the Ouija can be extremely useful. But it is understandable why controversy surrounds the Ouija board. For decades it hasn't been treated with the respect that it deserves, but instead is brought out at parties to summon spooks when the guests have all had too much to drink. On the big screen, it is sometimes depicted as a tool to muster some evil entity or other, and in a way those films have it half right: the Ouija is a basic form of divining tool, and with it you can, in all innocence, easily tap into the lower vibrations. Therefore, I think it is safe to say that you need to know what you are doing and gain some experience before you dabble.

THE MODERN TALKING BOARD

In the 1890s, an American novelty inventor named William Fuld made improvements to the talking board, which he began manufacturing under the name "Ouija." In 1966, the Fuld estate sold the Ouija patent to Parker Brothers and the board took on a new life, but this time as a popular parlor game. Still, the Ouija did retain its mystique as a kind of otherworldly portal for students of the spiritual. I have always believed there are people who want to know what is on the other side of the mountain, and then there are those people who want to know what is beyond the portal of death—people who are willing to reach out beyond their comfort zones and explore whole new dimensions of time and space. Those people are usually at the forefront of new ideas, movements, and trends, and so it came to pass that at the height of the hippie movement and the Age of Aquarius, the Ouija board became wildly popular. The Ouija trend was picked up in certain social circles, and ladies of means would hire mediums whose specialty was communicating with the departed. Newspapers and magazine articles poked fun at these "séance sitters." Dressed in their Sunday best, they would meet once a week at one another's homes, hoping to make contact with loved ones on the other side.

More importantly—though those sensationalizing tabloid writers overlooked it—these people were looking for hope. They wanted to believe that life did not end with death, that there was a greater purpose for being here. They also wanted to know how the Ouija board could bridge the gap between life and death. I don't think that's crazy or silly; I think that's the natural human state, to be curious and to want to know more about these things.

And what do *I* personally know about the subject? Well, have I got a story for you!

MY SÉANCE WITH SONIA

In the 1970s, an elderly woman named Sonia came to me, hoping for an answer to her question of whether or not there was a God. Her face and body showed the ravages of living through the horror of the Holocaust. Imprisoned in Bergen-Belsen, the notorious Nazi concentration camp in Germany, she had survived the most wretched conditions one could ever imagine. Sonia was forced into slave labor at an early age and watched helplessly as friends, family, and other loved ones were put to death in ways too gruesome to describe here.

She had heard about the strange and mysterious Ouija board and was willing to cast her skepticism aside to see what message this little talking board would reveal. I had never done a séance before, but I had certainly been working with my psychic gifts for some time, so I was willing to give it a whirl.

I invited Sonia to sit in my dining room and placed the Ouija board on the table. I turned off all the lights and lit a small white candle that I placed at the top of the board. I asked her to hold hands with me as I asked the universe the question: "Is there anyone here from the other side who wishes to communicate with those seated at the table?"

No answer. So I asked the question again, but this time, something happened that caused my heart to skip a beat. The white candle took on an orange glow and cast an eerie shadow on the board. We watched as the shadow took on the shape of a face. At that moment, I knew we were not alone in the room anymore. Someone, or some presence, was there.

Within seconds, the shadow from the flame appeared to float across the board, as if some unseen hand was guiding it to spell out a message. We watched in stunned silence as the candle stopped at the letter B. From there it traveled to the letter E, followed by L, I, E, V, and E again. The Ouija board had spelled out the word *believe*. Without warning, a cold breeze blew out the candle. I turned on the lights and asked Sonia if she knew what the message meant.

Tears rolled down her face. She explained to me that when the Gestapo came to take her and her family away to the camps, her father said, "Life is a challenge, a series of tests. Believe there is a reason for everything, and never stop believing that we won't be separated in death."

Sonia left that day *knowing* that her loved ones were safe and sound on the other side. But she is far from the only one to receive news from the spiritual plane. The Ouija has taught many life lessons to those fortunate enough to connect with it and "hear" the message that the world doesn't end here, that this life is just the beginning, a stairway to the stars and the door to a whole new dimension to explore.

CONDUCTING A OUIJA SÉANCE

If you have an interest in the Ouija board and would like to try your hand at contacting someone who has passed over, before you begin you should know that both the American and British boards are exactly the same, but with an added caveat. In America, the Ouija board is generally used for fun and bonding with friends, while in Europe, it is taken a little more seriously. The board does have to be treated with respect, and you must create the perfect peaceful ambience to ensure that the spirit you conjure is a good spirit and not one from a lower realm. As we mentioned in an earlier chapter, just as there are good and bad people in this world, there are also good and bad spirits. In order to attract only the positive souls, make sure to cleanse the room by burning incense and lighting a white candle before you begin and make sure your focus is clear and pure.

PREPARE TO MAKE CONTACT

Invite some friends over, enough to form a circle around a table. When your friends are all in position, you are ready to begin. Make sure there are no distractions in the room; ask everyone to turn off their cell phones, and make sure nobody needs to use the restroom. People often get nervous during the session, and you certainly don't want your work interrupted by a bathroom break. It's also common for some people to burst into fits of giggles. If this happens, you can offer the nervous laughers a calming glass of wine, but keep the alcohol consumption to a minimum; too much may affect their ability to focus.

Place your Ouija board on the table along with a white candle and a glass of water, which gives the spirits energy. Dim the lights, light the candle to begin, and follow these steps.

1. Ask everyone in the group to inhale for ten seconds and then exhale. Inhale ten seconds, exhale. Inhale ten seconds, exhale.
2. Now ask everyone to hold hands around the table.
3. In your own words, say a prayer for protection and ask the angels to encircle the room with only positive energy. Be assertive in your prayer; insist that only benevolent spirits are welcome, and demand that all others stay away.
4. After the prayer, remain silent for about two or three minutes and continue with your breathing.
5. Stay in the moment and apply your mind to the board. Take a deep breath and ask the universe

if there is anyone from the other side who wishes to make contact. You might be lucky on your first try and hear a distant knock. The knock might come from underneath the table, or it might be in the next room. It's perfectly normal to feel a little nervous when you hear these sounds, but try not to let on to your guests. Remain as calm as possible.

6. Tell all your guests to put their right index finger on the planchette. Now it is your job as the host of the séance to ask the board a yes-or-no question. If you do have a spirit present, the spirit will move the planchette, sliding it around to point to YES or NO on the board. If you ask a more complex question, the planchette will point to different letters on the board, which will go on to spell out names or places or significant words. Just remember, ghosts don't have spell-check on the other side, so be prepared to use your phonetic skills to decipher answers.

ENDING THE SÉANCE

If all has gone well, you will have received the information you asked for. This is where you thank the spirit sincerely for its time and sign off by moving the planchette over GOOD BYE on the bottom of the board.

Often a spirit summoned in Ouija practice will hang around, sometimes for days or weeks after a séance. Therefore, it is imperative that you close the session properly and send the spirit back. Prepare a little speech to use once you have moved your planchette over GOOD BYE and state clearly that you wish it to return to the place it came from. If this doesn't work and you find yourself haunted by a spirit's continuing presence, you can rectify the problem quickly and easily. First, take out the Ouija board again and apologize to the ghost. Acknowledge that you know it is around and that you are sorry it has failed to return home. Tell the ghost to go toward the light and to meet its guide there. Say to it that all the love is in the light and that it must depart the earth plane immediately.

The spirit may be confused after crossing over to the earth plane; with its guide beckoning it at one end and you pushing it out the door at the other, it is more likely to cross back. Close the session by saying again that the spirit's job is done and its presence is no longer required. This usually does the trick.

OUIJA FOR SELF-ENLIGHTENMENT

While the Ouija is an excellent tool for blurring the boundaries between the material and ethereal planes, you can also use it to learn more about your own heart, soul, and desires. This is a completely different practice from a séance; it is what we call spiritualism in a broader sense. To my knowledge, no one has used the Ouija board as a spiritual guide in the way I am going to reveal to you now.

People are drawn to tools like the Ouija for very diverse reasons, so I'm not going to assume that you are already on a spiritual quest just because you're interested in this type of magick. But I am going to talk about expanding your mind into this horizon, just in case you ever find yourself ready to go there. What I'm really talking about is developing your own sense of spiritualism, which is technically a religious endeavor, but one that I think describes the search for self and soul perfectly.

The important thing about spiritualism is that it teaches us that we all have two equally important aspects to our characters: the physical *and* the spiritual. One can't prosper without the other, and each must be nurtured if we are to have the healthiest life possible.

DISCOVER THE BEST OF YOURSELF

We are living at a time in which materialism has almost completely overtaken spiritualism. People have become disconnected from the rest of the world. The word *neighbor* has been replaced by the phrase *the person (or the stranger) who lives next door*. The homeless are looked upon as an annoying presence that we step over in the street, not as desperate people in need. The old, the sick, and the dying are just a burden on society, so why should we reach out and help them? Unless we change our perception of those less fortunate than ourselves, we are doomed to live in a callous world in which there is no hope for change.

The thing about not being in touch with your spiritual side is that you really don't know who you are and who you are capable of becoming. There may be aspects of your personality that you have no idea exist, and those aspects may be important not only to you as an individual, but to the entire world. That's the point of this exercise with the Ouija: finding those hidden, glorious parts of your soul that need illumination.

We have to understand that the time for change has come. You are the New Age generation that can make a difference in the world. It's time to step outside the box and inspire those who are not yet stimulated by intellectual curiosity.

THE PROCESS

It is very important before you start the process that you take your Ouija board in your hands and hold it to your chest. Sit quietly with it, breathing deeply. Do this for just a minute or two so the board can absorb your energies and thoughts.

Place the board on a table. Put your fingers on the planchette. In this method of consulting the Ouija board, you can ask only yes-or-no questions. Keep them simple to start, such as "Should I wear my blue sweater Saturday night?" You might feel a pull or tug to your left or right. That's great, because it means the planchette is responding to your energies. You've warmed it up and it's ready to work.

At this point, I want you to ask the board some more esoteric questions, such as "Is there a reason for my being here?" or "Do I have a special purpose in life?" You can even ask if the career you have will lead to success. What you are doing during this process is tuning in to your inner self. You see, the Ouija board can act as a bridge between you and your subconscious mind. In truth, you already know most, if not all, of the answers, and the Ouija board is just validating what you know.

Ask the board if you have a special mission in life to fulfill. Let's say, for argument's sake, that the planchette moves slightly to the right. (It does not have to touch the YES on top of the board; just a move in that direction is enough.) Okay, we now know you have a special purpose. Follow up that question by asking the board another question, such as "Do you mean helping people?" If the planchette moves again to the right, we now know that helping people is your mission in life. You can go on to ask another level of yes-or-no questions, such as "By volunteering?" or "By going into nursing?" or "By becoming a teacher?"

The true testament to the Ouija board's power comes when you ask deeper and more involved questions. This is when spiritualism and mysticism kick in. As you ask one question and receive an answer, it inevitably leads to another question, and another, and another.

What you are really doing is retraining your thinking, learning to get in touch with your inner voice or subconscious mind. This is an easy exercise, but it does require you to think on a level that you probably aren't in touch with on a day-to-day basis.

Share the Lessons

The Ouija board is a tool for enlightenment. Use the knowledge it gives you to help others who have lost their way in life. Tell them there is another road to take, less traveled, a road that will lead them to fulfillment within themselves. Guide them by example, maybe even giving them their own Ouija board as a gift of encouragement to explore a whole new world of possibilities. And, by your doing so, the Ouija board will live on for generations to come.

PART TWO

SPELL CASTING

AND

WITCHCRAFT

CHAPTER 4

LEANNA

MAGICKAL MOON

EVEN WITH THE TECHNOLOGY WE HAVE today, when you glance up at the sky on a clear night and see our fine-looking moon shining there in all its glory, you have to admit it's a pretty awesome sight. For thousands of years the moon has been seen as having a magickal presence, and even our ancestors believed that it had some spiritual significance. Although we now have a greater scientific understanding of the moon and its effect on Earth, most of the astronauts who have visited the moon have returned more in tune with their spiritual side and gone on to explore their religious or metaphysical beliefs in a deeper way.

MOON PHASES AND MAGICK

The next few pages list numerous spells that you can perform during different phases of the moon—certain spells work better during particular phases. All the spells listed can be cast in a simple ritual: Take a small white candle to the window and gaze at the moon through the windowpane. Say your wish out loud and with feeling, then leave the candle to burn down and blow out (while you are still in the room, of course; do not leave the candle unattended or place it near a curtain). If you prefer, you can refer to the other spells in this book, such as those using pouches and wish boxes (chapter 7) or text magick (chapter 6), and conduct them on the appropriate moon phase.

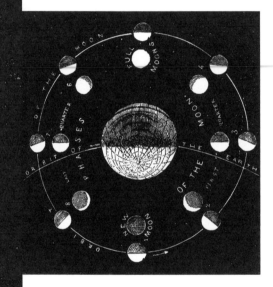

THE FULL MOON

At one time it was thought that the moon and its phases interfered with our internal chemistry by exerting gravitational forces on our bodies, or that the moon's gravitational fields caused electrical particles to fall to Earth, interfering with the complex functions of our brains. Recent scientific studies have disproved these theories, as well as invalidating the long-held belief that crimes and mental instability (hence the word *lunatic*) increase during full moons. In any event, from a magickal point of view the full moon does not have any negative connotations; it is just considered a very powerful time of the month. For some reason, Fridays that fall on full moons are wonderful days for casting love spells. If you try casting love spells during any other moon phase, it doesn't mean that they will not work, but the results could take much longer. There are lots of other spells that benefit from being cast on a full moon too, and these are listed below:

* Protecting property and home
* Adding vigor to your life
* Anything to do with love
* Increasing self-confidence
* Advancing in career and work
* Enhancing psychic ability/clairvoyance
* Strengthening friendships and family bonds
* Performing general good-luck spells

THE WAXING MOON

When the moon is waxing, witches like to cast spells for improving situations or for getting things going if things have been in a rut for a while. Often, when life is unchanging, it takes a little boost to amp things up a bit, and this phase is definitely the best time to kick-start your life. The following spells act faster during a waxing moon:

* Moving forward from depression
* Getting out of a rut
* Passing examinations and tests
* Finding lost objects
* Healing a sick animal or finding a lost pet

* Nurturing abundant, healthy gardens and the well-being of nature
* Losing weight or stopping smoking

THE WANING MOON

We all get into trouble at some point in our lives or face circumstances that are beyond our control. The waning moon is the perfect time to cast spells for getting rid of the black clouds and negative energies that sometimes hang over us. It is a time when you can draw down strength from the universe. If you are surrounded by difficult people and feel you can't cope, or if you have to tackle difficult situations head on, you can use the moon's power to assist you. By casting spells during this phase, you will gain the power to take control again, strengthen your weak areas, and become more assertive in your actions. Cast spells at this time for:

* Developing inner strength and assertiveness
* Banishing enemies
* Stopping arguments
* Soothing unruly children
* Calming anxiety
* Getting out of tricky situations

THE NEW MOON

This is my favorite lunar time, and it is appropriate for almost any spell. The new moon phase surrounds us with lots of positive energy and can act as a catalyst for immediate change. Many transitions naturally happen around a new moon anyway, such as new jobs, births, and moves, but if you need to revolutionize your life, cast spells at this time for:

* Career changes
* Moving house swiftly and easily
* Safe and enjoyable travel
* Increasing your cash flow
* Better health
* Conceiving

Women and the Moon

The moon was worshipped in many early religions as a goddess, and it has always been seen as a feminine symbol. On average, our big, beautiful moon orbits at a distance of approximately 238,855 miles from Earth and takes around 28 days to complete its orbit—interestingly, the same as the average amount of time between female menstrual cycles.

MOONS AND MOODS

If you get interested in studying the moon's patterns, you may find that your demeanor changes depending on what the moon is doing. I experimented with this once for a few months, keeping a note in my Book of Shadows about how I felt with each passing phase. It was fascinating to find that during the dark of the moon I was a bit irritable and absentminded, but once that phase had passed I cheered up and began to feel more grounded. Certain situations can naturally occur during certain phases, too. For example, the handyman came to repair my leaking roof on the first day of a new moon, so I instinctively knew that he would do a good job—and he did! Both my children were born on full moon phases, which makes me believe that they are psychically gifted and will probably go on to have an interest in all things magickal. Animals may also be affected by the full moon phase and can become a bit more rambunctious, so if you're a witch with felines, keep catnip at hand.

THE DARK OR VOID OF THE MOON

The dark moon, when the face of the moon is hidden, is also known as the "dead" moon. It takes place precisely three days before a new moon and is considered to be the most magickal and potent of all the phases. Sadly, many people who practice black magick do so at this time. You might think that someone working on the darker side of the occult could not influence any spells or rituals that you might be performing, but the collective power mustered by these individuals can cause cosmic havoc: our spells may become confused or simply not work at all. It is a shame, because the brilliance and power of this phase really is incredible, and without the negative manipulation I am sure we witches could do a great deal of good in it. That said, I often tell people that unless they are experienced wand wavers, it is probably best not to attempt any rituals at this time, but to wait until the new moon comes in. Speaking for myself, I never cast spells during a dark moon phase; I just hang up my cauldron for a few days.

Shawn's Tip

I never underestimate the power of the moon, and I always keep a note of what it is doing and when it is going to change. You can purchase a small diary with all the phases listed inside or go to the Internet and look up the information there.

SPELLS

AND

CANDLE
MAGICK

WHAT IS A SPELL AND HOW DOES IT work? I have been asked these questions many times over the years, and even today I still have trouble answering them.

I suppose you have to look at spells as a form of cosmic ordering—a form of thought projection. A thought is a very powerful thing, and when you project it outward into the cosmos in a spell, it is universally received and returned to you. Another theory is that a spell is a direct request to your personal guide or angel, who can choose to grant your wishes and fulfill your needs. We have all heard about the power of prayer, and spell casting is not so different. Our spirit helpers want us to connect with them, and they often assist us, even if we don't realize it. When we meditate properly and call for help, we are tapping into a spiritual portal and opening the gateway to receive their support.

As I have mentioned in other chapters, we are not born alone, nor do we die alone. Sometimes our spirit friends refrain from interfering with our lives because that might keep us from learning the valuable lessons we are destined to learn, but they will prop us up and lend a hand if they are allowed.

DO SPELLS ALWAYS WORK (AND IS IT REALLY SO EASY TO JUST GET WHAT YOU WANT)?

It is rare that we are granted our desires if our need is not genuine. So for those wanting to live in a big house and have oodles of money, with a hottie in bed next to you every morning—you may be disappointed! Spells usually work for the important things in life and tend to succeed best in crisis situations. So if you are truly desperate and your need is legitimate, calling on your spirit guides will help. That is not to say that you can't cast a spell for something trivial. I often cast spells to get a parking space simply by just saying out loud, "*I desire a parking space, so mote it be.*" This can also be used if you have lost something and need to find it in a hurry. Use the same wording: "*I desire to find (whatever you have lost), so mote it be.*" The main thing to remember is that spells that are cast halfheartedly usually don't work. You need to believe in what you are doing and have faith in yourself and your magick. If you truly believe that you are going to find your car keys, then you will.

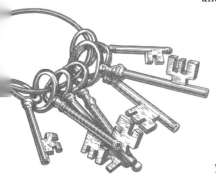

SHOUTING YOUR WISH

This may sound a little crazy, but when you yell out your wish to the universe, you can make things happen in an instant. (Although I do advise that you try out this technique when you are alone, or some people may assume that you *are* unbalanced.) Some years ago my mother's boiler decided to conk out, and as it was a Sunday, we knew it would be impossible to track down a plumber. It was bitter cold outside and we were shivering miserably, so in frustration she stood in front of the lifeless boiler and hollered, "I DESIRE FOR YOU TO WORK RIGHT NOW, SO MOTE IT BE." I was amazed when the boiler powered right up and the heat started to return to the radiators. Of course, it did break down again the next day and we did need the plumber, but it worked through that Sunday night to keep us warm and cozy. I began trying this technique in other situations and found it to work nearly every time. I suppose the pent-up emotions, twinned with a spell, send a very powerful message to the universe, and all those lovely spirit helpers can't help but hear you above anyone else!

THE CANDLE RITUAL

Candles have always played a major part in spell-casting rituals, and although it is perfectly acceptable to simply voice our needs and desires, sometimes spells carry much more potency when we focus on the issues with a flame or two. Fire is a powerful element, so when a spell is recited over a lit candle, the message is transported to the universe much more forcefully and the desire directed back to us in due course. In Wiccan circles, this is called a candle ritual or candle magick. Most Wiccans have a collection of candles in assorted colors for every occasion. Each candle color has its own significance and therefore tends to work better for a particular problem.

BASIC CANDLE COLORS
AND THEIR INFLUENCES

Gold, Orange, and Yellow
Healing, for both the mind and the body. Self-confidence and self-esteem. Fathers who may need a little help with parenting. Communication. Education. Finding lost property. Improving writing skills.

Silver and Blue
Increasing psychic abilities. Issues that have to do with home and family. Women, pregnancy, and motherhood. Safe travels.

Red
Confidence and courage. Increasing sexual energy. Arousing passion. Protection against being attacked; protection against rapists and domestic violence.

Purple
Protection in general. House blessings. Invoking spirits. Business and work issues. New jobs.

Pink
Encouraging romance and attracting love. Creating harmony in relationships and marriage. Enhancing beauty to appear more physically attractive. Improving musical talents.

Green
Successfully managing wealth and money (see spell on page 270). Nature and garden spells. Passing driving tests. Success and achievements.

Brown and Black

Banishing evil. Stopping harassment or bullying. For a swift transition when moving house. Strengthening self-discipline, such as when dieting or stopping smoking.

White

White candles can be used for anything at all, as white is a neutral color. You can replace any color candle with white if you don't know what color is the best for a specific spell or you don't have the right one on hand.

PREPARING YOUR CANDLE

Before you cast any spell with a candle, it is important to prepare the candle first. To begin, cleanse it by wiping it with a clean damp cloth. This will ensure that any unwanted energy is washed away. Take a sharp knife or pin and inscribe your desires onto the wax. Make the inscription as detailed as you can and as the length of the candle allows. It can be hard to fit long sentences on a small piece of candle, so inscriptions can be brief, just be sure it is clear what you want. For example, if I were to cast a spell for success in my career, I would inscribe my name and the words *"To be successful in my work."* You may find you need a little practice with your knife or pin to make your inscription legible (and take care not to cut yourself), but rest assured the angels have had many eons of practice at trying to decipher these scribbles and they will be able to read just about anything you write!

Anointing the candle with oil is the final stage of preparation. A witch with lots of experience in essential oils might use a special type, such as lavender or citronella, but commonly available vegetable oil is perfect for beginners and will work just as well. Dip your finger into a tiny drop of oil and run it around the base of the candle. Now it is time for the words of your spell, otherwise known as the incantation.

OPENING A SPELL

A good way to begin a spell is by doing something we call casting a circle. Once you have all the items you need on your altar, take hold of either a quartz crystal or your wand in your right hand and stand quietly in front of your work space for a moment or two. Wave the crystal or wand over your objects, making the shape of a large circle in the air. This will

enclose all of the magick inside the circle and keep out anything negative. There is no need to say anything at this point. In fact, I have found that if this is done in silence, it enhances the ritual without adding any confusing elements.

You can cast a circle either before or after you light the candle, but I recommend lighting the candle after you cast the circle so you don't risk setting your clothes on fire.

RHYMES AND REASONS AND MAGICKAL NUMBERS

Chanting the same thing over and over again is not an uncommon practice in most faiths. Repeated mantras put our minds in a trancelike state that helps us to tune in to the natural cosmic power around us. When following the spells in this book, you will notice that the instructions sometimes tell you to say an incantation seven, nine, or twelve times. These numbers play an important role in magick because they are highly spiritual and are thought to connect to the higher power more rapidly. When an incantation is repeated seven, nine, or twelve times, it works much better.

Once your candle is prepared, you light it and speak the incantation you inscribed on it, repeating the words seven times, as shown below. You can write anything you want on a candle, but this simple "I desire" spell holds a magick all its own. I have experimented with other words, such as "I wish," and haven't had the same results.

Returning to my example of wanting to be successful in my career, and using the words I inscribed, I would say:

I desire to be successful in my work.
I desire to be successful in my work.
I desire to be successful in my work.
I desire to be successful in my work.
I desire to be successful in my work.
I desire to be successful in my work.
I desire to be successful in my work.

It's traditional for spells to rhyme, like some poems or songs, though it is not necessary: if you are good at poetry, you may be able to write your own spells at some point.

A good example of a traditional rhyming spell is this one, often cast for bringing better health:

With magickal moon rays my soul is blessed,
Banish my pains and give me some rest.

The spells given in this book tell you how many times to say the incantation. If you write your own spells, try speaking your incantation seven times to begin with. For spells with shorter incantations, you can try nine or twelve times.

CLOSING A SPELL

When you have said your incantation over whichever spell you are casting, always close it down by saying the words "*So mote it be.*" Some witches like to say "*And so it is*" or "*The spell is cast,*" so go with whatever closing phrase you prefer. I like to say a silent thank-you to the angels too when I close a spell down, and I'm sure they smile down on me because of it.

Once you have followed these steps and your magick is under way, leave the candle to burn down and extinguish itself unless the instructions state otherwise. Some spells require you to blow out the flame earlier, but in general, it's best to leave it undisturbed and let it do its thing. (Note: Never leave burning candles unattended, and make sure the flames are not close to anything flammable.)

Shawn's Tip

The size of the candle is not important, but most rituals suggest that you allow the candle to burn all the way down, so it's best to use either a short taper or a tea light to reduce burning time. To inscribe a tea light, use a fine pin and keep the wording short.

The simple candle ritual outlined in this chapter works for almost any situation, and you can perform it even when you don't have much time. As the book goes on, we will cover many different spell-casting methods, but for now, a simple candle spell with a spoken incantation will get you started.

CELL PHONE SORCERY

AND

MICROWAVE MAGICK

I N TODAY'S WORLD, IT MIGHT SEEM STRANGE to think of someone not owning a cell phone, and it probably seems equally bizarre for a phone to be associated with magick and casting spells! So it may surprise some people to learn that high-tech gadgets and gizmos do have a very important place in a modern witch's toolbox.

Although there are some eccentric witches out there who still brew steaming potions in remote corners of forests, they really are quite a rare sight these days. We've gone mainstream, and most of us have cell phones. I remember when I purchased my first mobile phone some years ago; even before I'd figured out how to call someone, I was seeking ways in which I could use the device magickally. It didn't take me long to figure out that by transmitting my desires over the cellular network, I could turn all of my wishes into reality.

I can't take all the credit for this new way of spell-making. My trusted friend and coauthor, Shawn, helped me to try out many different ways of weaving together these contemporary spells, and after a few months of experimenting we figured out how to make the cell phone work to our advantage.

It's all in the power and intent of the message. We know, for example, that by sending a thought to the universe, we can attract the things we desire. Writing spells with pen and paper is a quick and easy way of getting what you want, but because of the energy that powers cell-phone towers and the speed with which we can send and receive texts, sending spells as text messages takes them to the next level.

Another easy aspect of spell texting is that you don't need candles or any other objects. All you need is a companion who also owns a cell phone and who knows you well enough to recognize that you are not completely mad! This person doesn't necessarily have to have any magickal know-how, just as long as they are open-minded and eager to experiment. In the past, I have known some witches who do this process alone by using two mobile devices, but in my opinion the spells work better if you actually enlist the help of another person.

DIGITAL MAGICK

This form of magick works for any situation, just as long as you keep things in perspective. As I suggested in the previous chapter, if you're aiming to be the next winner of the *Voice* or if you intend on spending the rest of your life with Bradley Cooper on a desert island, you could be sadly disappointed. Keep your requests reasonable and you shouldn't have any trouble at all. This is not rocket science. Whatever your dilemma or need, text a positive,

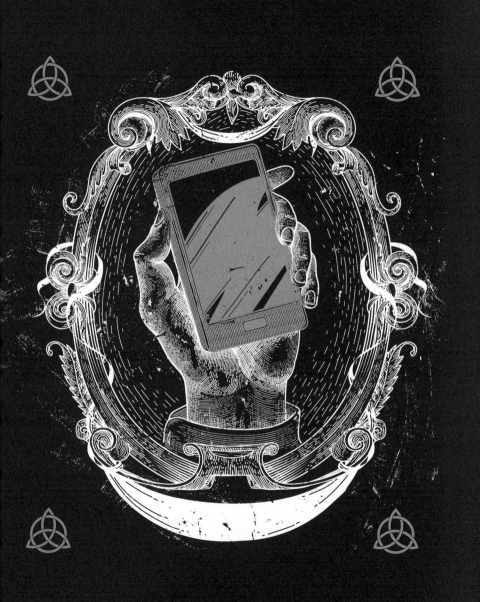

definite message and then visualize the outcome. State very clearly and simply exactly what it is you want. Finally, always close the spell by adding the words "*So mote it be.*"

TEXT POSITIVE

Let me give you an example of how to use text magick. If your friend wants a new job, text the words "*Susan Doe will get a fabulous new job soon. So mote it be.*" Send the text message to Susan's phone and tell her to read it but not to delete it. The message should not be deleted until the spell has worked. Often, it takes only one text message to get results, but you can send the same text every day for a week if you need to.

Let's look at another example: if you're not feeling well, ask a friend to cast a text spell to help you feel better. She will text your name and the words "*To feel better soon. So mote it be.*" Once again, open the message and leave it on your phone until your health has improved.

You may be astonished at the variety of things you can achieve using this simple and accessible form of spell casting! Shawn once helped a friend find his soul mate with text messaging. She sent a text to his phone wishing for him to find the lady of his dreams; within two weeks he met Elizabeth, and he is now happily married with three sons! And I once helped a friend who had a problem with noisy neighbors. Every night they would play loud music and throw rip-roaring parties. The poor woman was virtually beside herself. She hadn't slept properly for weeks, and the more she complained to them, the more they ramped up their speakers. This kind of disrespect makes me hopping mad, so I sent her a text message saying, "*I desire for your neighbors to move house within one month, so mote it be.*" Sure enough, within three weeks the town authorities had them evicted. She now has a nice, quiet older lady living next door and is quite content. However, as with all things magickal, some spells will work immediately, while others may take a little longer. Spells have their own magical timetable. You may have to repeat the spell for a week until your thoughts, wishes, and desires are granted. If you find that nothing has happened after a month or so, go ahead and repeat the spell.

E-MAILING SPELLS

In our early days of experimenting with text magick, I began to wonder if the same methods of spell casting would work with e-mails. This proved to be a little more complicated, but after a few months I started to get successful results.

Let's say for argument's sake that Susan Doe wants to meet the man of her dreams. To cast an e-mail spell, open a new e-mail and type "Love Spell" in the subject line. Next, type the spell seven times in the body of the message, as follows:

I desire for Susan Doe to meet the man of her dreams.

I desire for Susan Doe to meet the man of her dreams.

I desire for Susan Doe to meet the man of her dreams.

I desire for Susan Doe to meet
the man of her dreams.

I desire for Susan Doe to meet
the man of her dreams.

I desire for Susan Doe to meet
the man of her dreams.

I desire for Susan Doe to meet
the man of her dreams.
So mote it be.

Send the e-mail to Susan and ask her to send it back to you once she has opened it. When you receive it, open it and send it back to her again. This e-mail ping-pong must be done a total of seven times, as seven is a very significant number in the world of witchcraft. Within seven weeks, the spell should have worked and Susan should be snuggling up with her Adonis.

Don't delete the e-mails from your in-boxes until the spell has worked. As with text messages, you can you send e-mail spells to yourself, but they will be more successful if you send them back and forth with another person. Once again, you can use this method of magick for a wide range of situations:

* Increasing your money
* Improving your health
* Passing an exam
* Finding a new job
* Buying or selling a home

. . . or anything else you can dream up. Keep your intent sincere, give it a whirl, and watch what happens!

BOOTING UP SPELLS

We all recognize the sounds a computer makes when it's booting up and loading all the programs that make it work. But what many people don't know is that this boost of energy projects a force that is quite remarkable. The power that's generated when a computer is turned on comes in with such a rush that it's possible to cast a little magick in the time it takes your computer to boot up.

The best way to harness this power is to resort to our ancient methods of pen-and-paper magick. Take a sticky note and write your wish on it. As with text magick, make your wish clear, concise, and sincere. Stick the note on the monitor (the frame will do if you don't want to stick it on the screen itself) and power up your machine. Leave the note in place for ten minutes before removing it. Repeat every day for a week. Interestingly, I have found that this form of spell casting works better if you begin the ritual during a full moon phase. The combined energies of the computer and the full moon help to make the spell more dynamic. If you're desperate and can't wait for a full moon phase, don't worry, the spell will still work; it may just take a few days longer. You might also like to add a bit more vigor to the spell by putting a picture of yourself on your desktop. I do this all the time when I need something personal—it adds a boost of energy.

I am lucky enough to have quite a large desk in my office, and I have set aside a small part of it as an altar. Casting spells next to the computer works in conjunction with the electricity and enhances each spell's potential. Shawn got so excited when she tried this that she abandoned her regular altar and set it up permanently next to her hard drive!

MICROWAVEABLE MAGICK

I'll let you in on another little secret: we witches don't really bother with our cauldrons much these days. We have evolved with the times and we use our microwaves and convection ovens. Any spell that entails mixing or brewing concoctions can easily be done in a microwave. It takes less time and the end results are actually enhanced, mainly because of the powerful electrical energies that the microwave transmits. So instead of tossing your popcorn into the microwave tonight, try out these microwaveable spells for the house and home. They are fairly simple, meant to help get you in the swing of spell casting in the kitchen.

BLESS MY SPACE

To get rid of negative energies in your home or to cleanse the air after a heated argument, put two teaspoons of finely chopped lavender, one teaspoon of chopped thyme, a teaspoon of salt, and a cup of bottled water

in a microwaveable bowl. (Note: I suggest bottled water because it is typically purer than tap water. Tap is okay, but the ingredients need to be as refined as possible, with no fluoride added. You can use filtered water too.) Mix all the ingredients together and zap them in the microwave for one minute. Allow the mixture to cool, then add seven drops of lavender oil and the juice of half a lemon. Place the potion in a clean bowl and carry it into every room in your house or apartment while you repeat these words:

> *Sweetness be seen,*
> *This home is clean.*

When this is done, dig a hole in the garden and empty the potion into it. If you don't have a garden, you can bury the contents in a plant pot and leave it outside. Almost immediately you will notice that your home has a much better feel about it.

UNWANTED GUESTS, BEGONE!

This spell works great for keeping anything or anyone unwanted from entering your home, be it an evil spirit or an ex-boyfriend. Pour one cup of bottled water into a microwaveable bowl and zap it in the microwave for one minute. Once the water has boiled, repeat this spell three times:

> *Magickal water bless thee,*
> *Magickal water cleanse me.*

Let the water cool completely, then place two cloves of garlic—peeled or unpeeled, whichever you prefer—in the liquid and leave it to steep overnight. The next day, drain the water into a separate bowl, setting the garlic aside. Go to the front door of your home and rub one of the garlic cloves around the door frame. Sprinkle a few drops of the magickal water on the floor just inside the door. When this is done, dispose of the potion down the sink and say the words of the spell again three times. Throw away the remaining nubs of garlic.

TO STOP A COMPUTER ADDICTION

This spell is wonderful if you have a spouse or child who is addicted to computer games or Web surfing. On a new moon phase, take three red candles and light them somewhere in the kitchen. Next, chop a handful of fresh mint and place it in a microwaveable bowl. Add the peel and juice of one lemon (to stimulate the mind and senses) and mix in a cup of bottled water. Heat the mixture in the microwave for one minute. Take the bowl out of the microwave and place it next to the candles. Leave it for half an hour to cool down. Once the potion has cooled, take a piece of quartz crystal and pop it into the bowl. Say this spell three times, changing "he" to "she" depending on the person:

Aromatic citrus scent
Fill this space with good intent.
Wake the senses, inspire the mind,
New horizons he will find.

When you have said the spell three times, close in the usual way by saying:

So mote it be.

Let the candles burn down and extinguish themselves (not unattended, of course), but leave the bowl somewhere near the computer or in the person's room for two days. This magickal potion will stimulate their mind and heighten their senses and make them want to explore more about their life and environment.

TO BANISH FEELINGS OF LONELINESS

On a new moon phase, make a cup of chamomile tea, and while it is hot, add three spice cloves. Leave the tea to cool completely. On a yellow candle, inscribe your name and the words *"To banish feelings of loneliness."* Light the candle, place the tea in the microwave, and heat it for one minute. While the potion is cooking, say this incantation nine times:

In my solitude, I will be strong.
The days are swift
and the nights are not long.

When you have recited the spell, close it by saying:

So mote it be.

Leave the candle to burn down and extinguish itself, and when the magickal tea is cold, sprinkle a few drops of it outside your front door, and your back door if you have one. This is a lovely spell to do if your partner is serving in the armed forces or works far away, and it can be repeated every time you get that lonely pang.

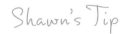

Shawn's Tip

Text these words into your phone: "I desire to spend the rest of my life on a desert island with Bradley Cooper, so mote it be." (Sorry, Leanna.) Hit the send button—there's nothing wrong with aiming high, and you never know, maybe this time the universe will listen!

Seriously, though—we all plug our cell phones into chargers at night to recharge them, but why not try a little magickal charging too? Draw the symbol of a pentagram on a piece of letter-size paper, place your phone in the center of the star, and leave it sitting there overnight. This will ensure that your phone will be chock-full of positive energy. Do this once a month.

MAGICK MODERNIZED

Witches of days gone by had to wait weeks for their spells to take effect—now we can harness the added energy of our phones and computers to boost the power of our thoughts, or pop a concoction into the microwave and nuke it. I think the fact that we can use these ultra-convenient gadgets is the ultimate testament to how magick evolves and changes with the times. That's good news for witches who are just getting started and great news for anyone who wants to see witchcraft thrive in the future.

WISH BOXES, POUCHES, AND HERBS

CREATING POUCHES AND WISH BOXES IS a lovely way of weaving magick to get your heart's desire. When you combine lots of objects and then cast a spell over them, you are merging their collective powers and bringing about a more intense ritual. A wish box can come in any shape or size. I like to buy the fancy boxes that you often get when you want to give someone a special gift, but a simple shoe box will suffice. The important thing is to decorate it beautifully: either cover it in pretty wrapping paper or, if you are creative enough, sketch or paint a design on the outside. Once you have the box ready to go, you can place all the necessary items inside to make your spell more effective.

Pouches or sachets are usually smaller and consist of a piece of material, about the size of a handkerchief, that holds the items. Once the objects are inside, the pouch is tied at the top with ribbon. You can carry it around with you or hang it above a door or bed, depending on its intended purpose.

Boxes and pouches are traditionally filled with herbs or spices. Many herbs and spices have unique magickal properties and, when used in conjunction with a spell, can make the ritual more effective and potent. To make sure you always know the right substances to use, it's important to keep a list of them and what they influence in your Book of Shadows. You'll find a list of the most commonly used herbs and spices in magick below. Fresh herbs are best, but the dried varieties are acceptable if fresh is not available. You can chop the herbs before placing them in the container or keep them whole; you can even tie the stemmed herbs in bundles and hang them up without using a box or pouch. When concoctions call for more than one element, you can add to their efficiency by mixing them together before you put them in your container. Be as inventive as you like, but just make sure that you have the correct herb or spice mixture for your spell. You can use the list below to make sure that you are choosing the right herbs and then blend them according to your specific desire. For example, if you want to conceive, you can combine basil (for babies) and heather (for good luck).

ANGELICA ROOT

The name gives it away—wonderful for summoning angels and asking for protection. Hang a pouch of this in the kitchen to bless your home.

BASIL

If you are trying to get pregnant, give your lucky man a thrill: hang a bunch of this above the bed and make love under it every night for two weeks. Basil is also commonly used in conjunction with money rituals to help boost income (see "The Money Pouch" in this chapter, on page 101, and "Using Citrine to Boost Cash Flow" in chapter 8, on page 105).

BAY
Take a handful of bay leaves and place them inside a wish box to remove curses. You can also sleep with a bay pouch under your pillow to facilitate lucid dreaming.

CATNIP
Carry catnip in your purse to attract love and popularity or to be safe when you are traveling. Witches often give catnip to their friends as a way of sealing the friendship and making sure it is long-lasting. (See "Poppy Seeds" for another way to use catnip.)

CHAMOMILE
If you suffer from bad dreams or insomnia, sprinkle a small amount of chamomile over your bedroom floor. This will induce sleep and ensure those dreams are sweet. I made pouches of chamomile and put them under my children's cribs when they were little to help them sleep through the night.

CHIVES
Tie a bunch of chives high above the front door to keep out unwanted spirits, or chop some finely with a knife and place them in a pouch to banish someone who is negative or harmful from your life.

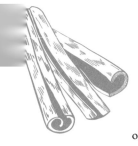

CINNAMON BARK OR POWDER

A very powerful herb, cinnamon is fantastic for increasing your psychic ability or helping with healing spells. To attract wealth, carry one stick or a tiny pouch of powder in your wallet.

CLOVES

If you are grieving, cloves will bring comfort to you. For help attracting Mr. or Ms. Right, push twenty cloves into a whole orange and pop it inside a wish box.

COMFREY LEAF

Chop up fresh comfrey leaves for protection during travel; it may help the purse strings too. Good to use in a spell for settling down emotions after times of stress or for securing a new job.

DANDELION LEAF OR ROOT

Dandelion has so many uses, it's impossible to list them all. For health and well-being, separate the petals from a few flowers and carry them on your person for a week. To summon the spirits and help with divination, take the root and place it in your wish box. If you rub the plant's sap on a wart, the wart will disappear.

DILL

When a baby is born, fill a pouch with freshly chopped dill and hang it above the nursery door. This will ensure that the child is protected and that he or she will grow up to succeed academically. Mix with lavender and elderflowers to attract romance.

ECHINACEA

Brilliant for keeping away colds and flu, so use in all healing spells for a little extra zing. Echinacea flowers can be used in a pouch to enhance meditation or scattered on the altar for money rituals.

ELDERBERRIES AND ELDERFLOWERS

Fill a pretty pouch with dried elderflower and give it to a bride on her wedding day to make sure she remains protected and happy in her marriage. Elder is great for any romantic purpose and works beautifully if used along with rose petals.

EUCALYPTUS LEAF

If the house has a heavy feel about it or the kids are constantly bickering, use eucalyptus leaves to calm down the disruptive energies. It's also excellent when used alongside sage to ward off illness.

FEVERFEW

This herb is renowned for getting rid of headaches, but it is also beneficial for clearing your head if you have decisions to make. The best magickal feverfew is grown outside, but be warned: plant it in a pot, for it can spread rapidly if left unrestrained in your garden.

GARLIC

I doubt you will be associating with vampires, but should you happen to come across one on your travels, garlic works as a great source of protection. Hang the bulbs in doorways to ward off evil or put garlic salt in pouches and sachets to keep away any bad vibrations.

HEATHER

Heather is a very lucky herb to have in the home, and when it is hung in a window it is said to bring good fortune to the people who live there. If you feel unsafe, or if you want to try something risky like bungee jumping or skydiving, carry a few sprigs on you and you'll automatically have protection.

LAVENDER

Lavender is incorporated a lot in spell casting and has many uses; the main one is to bring a sense of calm to situations and to promote peaceful sleep. To attract a partner, carry some lavender and a piece of amethyst crystal together. They complement each other and enhance any love spell.

MANDRAKE ROOT

The mandrake root has been considered a powerful talisman since biblical times. It has long been used in witchcraft to guard against any kind of misfortune. If you have had a run of bad luck, hang a pouch of mandrake in the living area of your home and it will absorb the negativity, leaving everything neutral again. If placed on your altar, the root will enhance your magickal workings and give your spells more power.

MINT

Angels and spirits are thought to love the smell of mint, so to encourage them into your life, grow mint in the garden and cut a few bunches every now and then to bring into the house.

MISTLETOE

Just because it's hung above doorways at Christmas doesn't mean you actually want to kiss everyone who stands under it. Traditionally mistletoe was used for encouraging love and fertility, but it has other qualities too. To distance yourself from annoying people, separate the berries from the stem and dry them before placing them in a wish box or sachet. Also works in warding off illness.

MUGWORT

I use mugwort in nearly every spell that I cast because it boosts the spell's performance and adds a bit of extra clout. Best used for scrying, divination, and prophetic dreams.

NETTLE

If your house is haunted, nettles will drive out unwanted spirits or deflect any curses. Carefully mix nettle with mandrake to make it more powerful—but wear gloves, because nettles do sting when they come in contact with the skin.

OAK BARK

Everyone has those times in life when they need a bit of extra physical or emotional strength. Use a small piece of bark in a pouch or a box to raise your energy level and put a spring back in your step.

POPPY SEEDS

These are great for love and fertility spells and perfect for pouches. During a full moon phase, take about a teaspoon of packaged poppy seeds and put them in a sachet with a teaspoon of catnip.

ROSEMARY

Probably one of the most widely used herbs in Wicca, rosemary is good for the soul and is treated as a powerful cleanser. Use it for house blessings or mix it with mint to prepare a magickal space for a spell.

SAGE

This herb promotes wisdom and knowledge, so it is helpful to use when you have an examination or a driving test coming up. Native Americans use smudge sticks made from white sage to purify their environments, and witches have adopted this method for clearing away bad vibes. White or common sage can be used.

SAINT-JOHN'S-WORT

Magickally speaking, this herb is a wonderful protection against fire. Banish ghosts and demons by hanging a pouch of Saint-John's-wort in a high spot in the house. It also promotes psychic vision and helps you foretell the future.

VALERIAN

Fresh valerian is not an easy herb to get hold of, but you can buy it on the Internet. In some countries, valerian is available only in powdered root form, sold in capsules in health food stores; you can use this as an alternative if the leaves are hard to come by. Placed in a wish box, valerian can ease tension and arguments. Animal spells benefit from valerian too, so if you have a problem with a pet, put some valerian on your altar.

VERVAIN

Get your wallet bursting with cash by carrying vervain in a sachet. It is also good for building up a business or seeking a promotion or a new job.

MAKING THE CONTAINERS

When you create any magickal box, it's essential that you write down exactly what you want on a piece of clean white paper. For instance, if you wanted to give a wish box to a newly married couple, you would write something like *"I desire for this union to be filled with happiness, love, and longevity. So mote it be."* Fold the paper in half, and then in half again, and place it inside the box or pouch.

It doesn't matter whether you leave your herbs in their original form as sprigs or whether you chop them. Just place your selection of herbs inside the box along with the folded paper and close the lid. If you are using a pouch, tie it up securely by either binding the top with a ribbon or pulling the drawstring tight. Once your box or pouch is filled and sealed, it is important that you charge its contents. On a clear night (making sure to avoid the dark of the moon), leave the box or sachet outside to soak up the moon's rays. The next morning, bring it inside and place it on your altar. Light a white candle and say this invocation nine times:

My magickal package is charged by the moon,
The wishes will be granted soon.

Leave the candle to burn for an hour before blowing it out. Then put your box in a safe place, or hang your pouch or carry it around with you. Once your wish has been granted, there is no need to discard your box or pouch. You can use it again in the future.

SPECIAL BOXES AND POUCHES

Whatever your wish or desire, you can make one of these magickal boxes or pouches very easily. Just be sure to use the right herbs for the situation at hand. Many herbs are good at helping to treat a variety of situations, so experiment with a few different types. You may find that one herb works better for you than another. Follow your intuition and go with what feels right in your heart. Make sure you record the results in your Book of Shadows so that you remember what works well and what needs fine-tuning. You can try these ready-to-use pouch and wish box "recipes" to start.

THE LOVE POUCH

If you want to attract a new partner, take a large white handkerchief and in the center place a needle threaded with red cotton, a small seashell, a teaspoon of poppy seeds, and some chopped lavender. On a small piece of paper, write your name and the words "*To attract a nice new lover.*" Gather up all four corners and tie the pouch with a red ribbon. Squirt the pouch with your favorite perfume and charge it under the moon. Carry the love pouch with you every time you go out and that handsome stranger will make an appearance very soon.

WISH BOX FOR GOOD HEALTH

If you are feeling under the weather or someone you know has had surgery, you can create a box to dispel sickness. Take your decorated box and place a photograph of the sick person inside, along with three sprigs of rosemary, a piece of oak bark, and a small piece of amethyst crystal. Write the name of the sufferer on a piece of paper, and then write the words "*With this spell, I/he/she will be well*" seven times. Fold the paper in half twice and place it in the box. Put the lid on and charge the box overnight. If the wish box is for someone else, give it to that person the very same day and tell them to keep it in a safe place until they feel better.

THE MONEY POUCH

To boost your finances, take a piece of green material the size of a handkerchief and in the center place three coins (any currency is fine), a small magnet, and a handful of chopped or dried basil. Write on a piece of paper your name and the words *"Money luck"* or the exact amount of money you need. Gather the corners together and tie with a green ribbon. Charge the pouch and then hang it somewhere in your kitchen. Little sums of money should start to appear within a few days.

ENEMY-BANISHING POUCH

If you want to remove someone from your life forever, take a piece of white material and place in the center a handful of fresh or dried sage, a teaspoon of mugwort, and a whole garlic bulb. Write on a piece of paper the name of the person you want to be rid of and the word *"Banish."* Gather the corners and tie the pouch with a purple ribbon. Charge the pouch and then hang it above your front door. To really make sure that the person never makes an appearance again, you can make three of these pouches and hang them around your home.

Shawn's Tip

I like to put a pouch of dried mint inside my pillowcase at night. It's great for meditation and helps me clear my mind. You can also blend it with lavender for restful sleep.

CRYSTAL POWER

WITCHES ALWAYS HAVE CRYSTALS somewhere on their person, and if you stroll around their gardens you will often find a piece of amethyst twinkling out at you from a cabbage patch, or perhaps there will be a sliver of quartz nestled somewhere under a bush. Because crystals possess unique properties of conductivity and electrical frequency, they are used in everything from radios to watches to computers. Wiccans value crystals because they are wonderful for changing auras from negative to positive and they help clear destructive energies from our homes and gardens. There are so many types of crystals in the world that it is impossible to list them all here. If you want to learn more about crystals, there are countless books and websites out there, but for now, I have listed the nine most common stones that witches tend to use on a daily basis.

These are not just worn as jewelry, but often placed on our altars to support a spell. You can use any size crystal or stone in a spell; the results will be the same.

Leanna's Tip

You should wash your crystals once a week or so. Crystals can absorb energies around them, so just as we need to wash to stay clean, you need to wash your crystals. You can put them in the bath with you (to be cleansed of external energies and infused with yours) or simply soak them in a bowl of water.

AMETHYST

This lavender-purple crystal has a gentle vibration and can be used for healing or to help calm stress and nerves. Amethyst can be placed near the stressed or ailing person or worn next to the skin. After the crystal has been worn for a week, rinse the stone in tepid water every evening for seven days and then let dry it overnight. When the healing process is done, leave the crystal overnight in the garden on a full or new moon to recharge it.

USING AMETHYST FOR HEALING

Here is another way to use amethyst if you are not feeling well: Pull the top covers back from your bed and place a small piece of amethyst on each corner.

Climb into bed and put the covers back over you, taking care not to shift the amethysts. Lie still on your back, close your eyes, and visualize the healing energies of the crystals radiating from the corners of the mattress. If you can, try to take a nap; when you wake, the crystals will have energized you. At bedtime, remove the crystals and place them under your pillow. Keep repeating this until you feel better.

CITRINE

The "cuddle quartz," as it is often called, carries the energy and colors of the sun. It is a harmonizing stone that can make you feel at peace with the world. If you are lonely, hold a piece of citrine and feel the energy of love come into your soul. If you are angry with someone and want to vent your spleen, then citrine will calm you. When witches want a bit more money energy, they use citrine along with money spells. This is the stone of abundance, good luck, and inspiration, so keep a piece on you at all times and you will never have to worry about paying your bills!

USING CITRINE TO BOOST CASH FLOW

Invite money into your life by setting up an altar and putting your bank statement or checkbook, your wallet, and some coins beside a lit green candle. Take a small piece of citrine and place this on top of the wallet. Write the words *"Money luck"* on a small piece of paper and leave this next to the bank statement. Once the candle has burned

down, leave everything undisturbed for nine hours and then place the crystal and the piece of paper inside your wallet. Within a few weeks, you should notice that your bank balance is much healthier.

HEMATITE

This shiny black, slate-gray, or silvery-red mineral is used for safety during astral travel and to ground you once your spirit returns to your body. This crystal is very good for people with circulatory problems or anemia. It's also excellent for memory and mental stimulation, so witches wear hematite while performing spells that may be difficult or lengthy. If you were a witch in a previous life, by wearing hematite you may be able to tap into a previous existence and drum up some of the old spells and potions you used in the past.

USING HEMATITE TO REDISCOVER PAST LIVES

On a rainy day, leave a piece of hematite outdoors for a few hours. This will increase its power and cleanse it, leaving it ready for use. That evening, carry or wear the stone, allowing it to tune in to your vibration. At bedtime, go to sleep holding it in your hand. As you drift off, ask the angels to open your mind and permit you to take a peek into your past existence. You may have a vision or dream of another lifetime.

LAPIS LAZULI

This rich blue stone has been treasured throughout history, from Egyptian pharaohs and Babylonian kings to Renaissance painters who ground the precious material themselves to create vibrant ultramarine pigments. Lapis is still held in high esteem by witches, and we are very respectful of its powerful energy. It wards off negative vibrations and, if worn at bedtime, can bring vivid dreams of other lives and links to soul mates who may not have reincarnated at this time and who decided to remain in the spirit world. Lapis alleviates migraines and problems with the throat, and it helps with ear infections too. But its main effect is to bring inner knowledge of other worlds. If you are seeking to enhance your psychic abilities, always wear this stone in jewelry form, and your insight will naturally develop.

USING LAPIS LAZULI TO INCREASE YOUR WISDOM

If you would like to become more intuitive or you want to develop your psychic abilities, purchase either a lapis lazuli necklace or a pair of earrings (because these will be near the head chakras and thus work better than a bracelet or ring) and make sure that no one but you wears your lapis. On a full moon, charge and bless your jewelry by leaving it outside in a bowl of salt water overnight. The next morning, dry it off, place it on your altar, and light a purple candle next to it. Recite this spell three times:

My inner wisdom shines like the sun,
All my visions have begun,
I see now what I did not before,
With every day, I notice more.

When you have recited the spell three times, say:

So mote it be.

Leave the candle to burn all the way down and blow itself out. Next, put on your jewelry and don't take it off for a week. Your instincts will be much sharper and your dreams more vivid.

MOLDAVITE

Although there is no absolute proof, this rare and precious natural glass gem, bottle-green in color, is thought to be extraterrestrial, formed from a meteorite impact. Because there is only a small, finite source of moldavite in Central Europe, it is sought after and rather expensive to purchase. You will have to be very grounded in order to wear this stone, because its power can easily overwhelm more sensitive individuals. I use moldavite often to enhance my psychic ability or to connect with my guides in dreams.

USING MOLDAVITE TO ENHANCE YOUR PSYCHIC GIFTS

Sit quietly in a room free of noise and clutter and hold a piece of moldavite in your left hand (nearest your heart). Close your eyes and concentrate on how the crystal feels in your palm. If the stone can help you, you will begin to feel a pulsating throb run through your fingers. At this point, place the stone in your pocket or, if it's a piece of jewelry, put it on. You will start to receive premonitions within a few hours. These can appear as imaginary visions or as significant dreams. Make sure to write them down.

MOONSTONE

Connected to the moon and its lunar phases, moonstone is a very mystical crystal. It has depth and translucency and is used to encourage premonitions during dreams. When you practice tarot or tea-leaf divination, you can wear moonstone earrings and rings to increase your psychic powers. This is a very feminine crystal, linked to the reproductive organs, the menstrual cycle, and female hormones. It can also be useful to help restore anyone who has gone into shock, or simply to calm volatile energies. I used this crystal on my first child to relax him when he was younger (see instructions below).

USING MOONSTONE TO CALM A CHILD

Lay a photograph of your child on your altar. Next to the photograph, light a candle—pink for a girl or blue for a boy. Place a piece of moonstone on top of the photograph and say this spell three times (using "her" or "him" as appropriate):

Let the fury in her heart subside,
Settle down her soul.
Swathe magick all around this child,
Make her spirit calm and mild.

When you have said the spell three times, close it by saying:

So mote it be.

Let the candle burn down and then remove the crystal and put it on a high shelf in the house. Your little one should settle down and become much sweeter in a few days.

QUARTZ (CLEAR)

Quartz is one of the most common minerals on earth, but it is considered an essential part of any witch's crystal collection. It is a multipurpose stone that can be included in almost any spell to bring about a positive result. Quartz is wonderful for balancing emotions, especially if you are trying to heal painful feelings such as child abuse issues or if you have problems with self-esteem. This crystal amplifies magickal wishes and will bring extra power to any spell. Use it to tap into a higher consciousness and to keep in touch with your spiritual side.

USING QUARTZ TO EASE UNHAPPINESS

If you are feeling out of sorts or can't shake off a sadness, try this simple spell to lift your spirits. During a new moon phase, take a piece of clear quartz and place it on a bed of sea salt, either on a small plate or in a bowl. Light a white candle next to it and say this spell nine times:

Painful feelings leave me,
Bring joy and pleasure swiftly.
Angels heal my suffering,
Light up my heart with speed.

When you have said the spell nine times, close by saying:

So mote it be.

Let the candle burn for one hour before blowing it out. Repeat every day until the candle has burned down.

ROSE QUARTZ

Pale pink and related to all things romantic, rose quartz sweetens one's mood and brings a calming influence to jittery brides and grooms. Witches use it to attract a beloved to themselves in spellcraft. When a witch is handfasted, she often carries a wand with a piece of this stone attached somewhere on the tip (see chapter 11, "Handfastings").

USING ROSE QUARTZ TO EASE NERVOUSNESS

If you are feeling on edge, go outside on a dry day with a cup of table salt to a place where you will not be disturbed. Scatter the salt in a large circle around you and place the rose quartz in the center. Turn around three times on the spot and look up at the sky. Silently ask the angels to bless the stone with calm energies. Then go about your usual business and retrieve the crystal in the evening. Carry it in your pocket or on your person at all times. If you have an especially bad attack of nerves, stand inside the circle of salt and ask the angels again to calm you down.

TURQUOISE

Turquoise is used mainly to ward off the evil eye or to protect yourself from negative people or influences. If you feel threatened in any way, use turquoise as an amulet. It can also purify the air and clear out heavy spiritual clutter. Turquoise is good to use if you have moved into a new home, to balance the energies and clear any negativity left behind by the previous inhabitants. I often carry a piece of turquoise with me as a protective measure when traveling. It is a very powerful crystal and a must in a white witch's collection.

USING TURQUOISE FOR PROTECTION WHEN TRAVELING

If you are handy with a needle, take a small piece of turquoise and stitch it into the hem of your pants or skirt. This will create a protective force field around you. You can also put a piece in a zipped compartment of your purse or in an inside pocket of your jacket. Recharge the turquoise every three weeks by adding it to your bathwater while you are bathing.

Shawn's Tip

You will probably acquire many different types of crystals and stones over time, and each has its place when being used in accordance with magick. When the crystals are not in use, just be sure to respect them. Keep them in a special velvet-lined box or some other luxurious container. Your crystals will work for a lifetime, so keep them safe and pampered and they will never let you down.

A WITCH'S MENAGERIE

I F YOU ARE A WITCHY TYPE OF PERSON, IT would be seriously unusual for you *not* to love animals. Most witches have an affinity for all things living and love nature very much. At the last count I had four cats, three dogs, a flock of hens, and a toad. Okay, so maybe you are not as animal-mad as I am, but a true witch will endeavor to have at least one critter as a companion in their lifetime. Not only do we love our pets, we also understand the importance of the animal kingdom in general. We believe that every creature from a tiny ant to a hefty hippo is as important as, if not more so than, we mere human beings are.

Our animals don't have the ability to verbally tell us when they are sick, fearful, or unhappy. Therefore, we must try and tune in to their vibrations and take care of them, making sure that they are well treated and never abused. This means that we need to show patience and kindness and the utmost respect to the animals in our lives. In this chapter you will discover the significant magickal characteristics of the birds, animals, and insects a witch should know and be aware of so she knows when nature is trying to send her important messages.

Omnivore or Vegetarian?

Although some Wiccans do become vegetarians, from a logical point of view many witches believe that the cycles of nature create a balance and a harmony on our planet, so to eat meat is absolutely fine as long as it is killed and prepared humanely. Personally, I would never consider eating any meat that wasn't free-range or organic, and although I realize that not everyone can afford such luxuries, if you can, it is always best.

FEATHERED FRIENDS

BLACKBIRD
In Wiccan circles blackbirds are greatly cherished as they are thought to be very psychic. When you see a blackbird singing just for you and she looks you straight in the eye, rush out and buy some sexy underwear as love is on its way to you.

BLUE TIT

The blue tit is a little bird that brings happiness and news of births and weddings. If you have these birds in your garden then everything will grow in abundance. If you see a scruffy, bedraggled little tit on your bird feeder (maybe he's old, dishevelled and past his use-by date) blow him a kiss and he'll live another year.

CROW

The wise crow is especially attracted to spiritual people. Witches and crows go together like bees and honey. If you throw out some corn, a crow will probably eat it and may hang around your home. They are extremely intelligent; some scientists who study crows have discovered astounding tool-making and problem-solving abilities in these birds. In England we are very superstitious about crows, and although the birds are considered noisy pests by some, Wiccans hold crows in high regard as spiritual messengers. You'll often see a crow pictured in tarot-card illustrations, sometimes perched on the shoulder of a witch.

CUCKOO

When you hear the first cuckoo call in the spring, quickly make a wish and it will be granted. This elusive bird is considered good luck, and to see one means that cash will soon be injected into your life.

FINCH

A finch is a truth seeker. It will ruffle its feathers if you are not being honest with yourself. You can also tell him your troubles and he will fly away with your problems, leaving them to disappear in the clouds.

MAGPIE

In the past, this poor bird has been almost universally maligned. People grumble that magpies kill other birds, take eggs from nesting songbirds, and steal bright and shiny objects. (Actually, so do crows, ravens, jays, and jackdaws, but those birds typically don't get the same reputation.) Wiccans choose not to alienate magpies because of some bad press. Chinese witches consider them beautiful and say they are half raven, half dove. These highly intelligent birds are often attracted to "spiritually blessed" places, so if you see one in your garden, you'll know your home and property are protected.

OWL

This wise bird, also known as "the fortune-teller," is said to hold all the secrets of the universe. Speak aloud to the owl and ask your question. If it hoots once, the answer will be no, but if it hoots twice, the answer will be yes. If this bird enters your house, it is thought to be a very bad omen. If you see its image on a window where it might have accidentally collided with the glass, this is news of a death.

PHEASANT

Of course, only I would have a pet pheasant! This is a bird of protection against dangers, especially for young people. If a wild pheasant is seen around a property where a child dwells, it is thought that the child will always be protected from danger. Witches often collect pheasant feathers and sew them into their costumes or the brims of their hats. I actually do have a wild pet pheasant, called Clive, who happily lives alongside my flock of hens. He beds down with them each night and taps his beak on the cat flap in the mornings for his corn. Pheasants are not very clever, though, so you have to be patient with them.

ROBIN
This charming little bird is loved by all, and its image graces many Yuletide cards. In Christianity, it is thought that the robin gained its red breast from the blood of Jesus after it plucked the deepest thorn from Jesus's brow when he was dying on the cross. You can speak to the robin if you are out and about in your garden; the bird may follow you around and might even land on your rake or spade. If a robin is a regular visitor to your garden, this is considered to be very lucky; but should it venture into the house unexpectedly, just like the owl, it portends some sad news on its way or even news of a death.

SPARROW
If a sparrow should fly at you, it could be a warning to look after your health.

SPARROW HAWK
When this bird makes direct eye contact with you, it is trying to impart news to you. Try to tune in to the sparrow hawk for its understanding and knowledge.

SWALLOW

If a swallow nests in the eaves of your house, then your property will be protected against bad weather.

WOODPECKER

Witches believe this bird has magickal powers and is the sentry or the guardian of all trees. If you catch some of the dust from a hole a woodpecker has been drilling, this can be used in spells to bring about happier times.

WREN

In ancient myth, the wren was often referred to as "the king of birds." Normally it's not a good omen to have a bird fly into your home, but should the wren stop in for a visit, it will leave behind magick and good luck. Usually, after the appearance of a wren, something wonderful will happen. They are difficult to shoo out of the house, though, and can be stubborn about when to leave.

FURRY FAMILIARS

BADGER

The badger is from the weasel family, and is a lunar animal. Lunar animals are magickal creatures associated with lunar goddesses, and there are many. The badger is said to possess supernatural powers and can sense when it is in the presence of a witch. If your garden is planted on magickal ley lines—thought to be paths of spiritual energy running through the earth along which ancient monuments were built and sacred sites aligned—the badger will be attracted to that force and visit nightly. For many years we have had a set of badgers visiting us, and their intelligence is remarkable.

BAT

Forever connected to all things spooky, this little winged creature can usually be found nearby wherever a witch resides. In Chinese folklore, bats have always been considered extremely auspicious, and should they nest under your roof, it is a sign of better things to come.

DOGS

We all know that when you own one, it's like having another child! But what many people don't realize is that dogs can be incredibly psychic. We have all heard stories about lost dogs traveling miles to return home or canines anticipating their owners' arrival when the owners are still a ways off. The latter could have to do with the fact that dogs have acute hearing and can detect the sound of a known vehicle, but it's also possible that dogs are psychically tuned in to their owners and can use their senses to detect the humans' emotions. Dogs are also sensitive to weather changes. So if a storm is brewing and you are out in the wilderness, follow your four-legged friend—he'll take you to safety.

FROGS, TOADS, AND NEWTS

Many "garden witches"—those who are steeped in the magickal lore and medicinal properties of herbs—will keep one or more of these amphibians as pets. I have a big, knobbly brown toad called Tiptoe, who adopted me some time ago. She lives in my greenhouse and keeps most of the bugs away. I do have to watch where I am treading, though, because she has this awful habit of camouflaging herself in the paving slabs. Last year she kept venturing into the house, and she took a fond liking to the cats' litter box. One day while emptying the litter box, I very nearly flushed Tiptoe down the toilet! Both frogs and toads are lucky to have around, but if one should be killed or be found dead on your property, then sad news of the loss of a friend is on its way to you.

HARE

The hare is another lunar creature revered by the Wiccan community. In the past, the pagans worshiped this animal, as it represented fertility and a new beginning. Many witches keep a hare ornament in their home or wear jewelry embellished with the image of a hare. "Star-gazing hares" are said to be attracted to the full moon and stars and are purported to be the most magickal as they are moon worshippers. If you see one, it is considered to be very good luck indeed. In my lifetime I have seen two, and on both occasions something magickal followed.

HORSE

The horse may be the only creature on the planet that has a problem with witches. It is a sensitive beast and has a very different vibration from ours. A Wiccan vibration can freak a horse out at times, so you have to be sympathetic and handle it carefully. Many horses become very skittish and frisky around Wiccans, often rearing up or neighing loudly. This really isn't the horse's fault; it can sense the psychic energies of the witch, and because it doesn't understand, it becomes anxious. Once a horse settles down a bit and gets used to you, a true friendship can be made. Every time I am in the presence of a horse, it curls his top lip up at me. I used to take it personally, but now I just curl mine back!

RABBIT

Another lunar creature. If a rabbit is found in your garden, it could mean news of a baby for you or someone close to you.

INSIGHTFUL INSECTS

BEE

These creatures are much treasured, and without them our world would not exist in the way we know it now. Witches often keep beehives because they love the natural ingredients found in honey, and they often use this nectar in healing potions. "Bee witches"—witches who keep bees—make sure the correct flowers and plants are available for these "little priests" of our gardens.

You should never swear in front of a bee; they are thought to weaken in the presence of negativity. If one should fly into the palm of your hand, legend has it that you'll soon receive money. If a bee doesn't like your energy, yeah, you guessed it—you get stung!

HORNET OR WASP

I may love all animals, and these insects may look very similar to bees, but I have to admit that hornets and wasps are annoying pests. Believe it or not, you can use telepathy with them, and if you tune in correctly, they will do as you ask. If a wasp or a hornet is aggravating you, speak to it firmly and say, "Please leave." Usually it will obey this command; if you get stung instead, it's a warning that there may be a person around you whom you should not trust. Jealousy is associated with hornets as well, so be on your guard.

A few years ago we had a nest of hornets in our eaves, and one flew into my bedroom. After speaking to it severely without any success, I glugged a mouthful of red wine and prepared myself for a fight. The hornet was clearly not happy, and it proceeded to dive-bomb me. With rolled-up newspaper in hand, I gave it a gentle bop on the head and it landed with a plop in my half-full wineglass. Panicking for a moment, I opened my bedroom window and threw the wasp and wine into the night. The next thing I heard was a "thump, thump, thump," and when I looked down, I saw that I had covered my beautiful blond pet rabbit in California Merlot!

GRASSHOPPER

If you happen to come face-to-face with a grasshopper, you will have to make a decision about a journey that lies ahead of you.

LADYBUG

The ladybug, or ladybird beetle, is a witch's little familiar; if one lands on you, many blessings will come. Hold it in your cupped hand for a few seconds and tell it your secrets. Then make a wish and let it go.

SPIDER

For better or worse, spiders of all shapes and sizes are attracted to witches like we're magnets. They'll run over our clothes, land on us when we least expect it, and even creep into bed with us! Okay, so they are not pretty—they have eight hairy legs, fat little bodies, and beady eyes—but they can't help the fact that they find us attractive. The spider, which is not strictly an insect—it is an invertebrate arthropod with an exoskeleton—is said to be the only living creature on the planet that can understand the human language. Some witches talk to spiders, and some are known to put one in their pocket for a few moments to increase their wealth (not *this* witch, though! I'd rather be poor, thank you very much). Never kill a spider intentionally—it's very bad luck, and if you do, you'll have a year of hardship. If you want to remove a spider from your space, try to dispose of it in a gentle way; despite its appearance, a spider is very vulnerable and easily upset. On a lighter note, if a tiny spider lands on you (this is okay, I can cope with the little ones), circle it three times over your head and let it drop into your hair. As odd as it sounds, just leave it there to find its own way out. This will increase your money energy three times over.

Shawn's Tip

If you have creatures in your house, such as ants, roaches, or mice, that you would like to "disinvite," ask them nicely but firmly to leave and they should soon make haste.

LEAVING THE BEST FOR LAST: CAT

Some of you may have noticed one glaring omission from my list of helpful creatures. Well, here it is—I always like to leave the best for last!

Would any picture of a witch be complete without the usual cat in attendance? Everybody knows cats are the most popular companions of witches, and if you don't know already, I am kind of cat-mad. I have four of the little furry beauties, and I am handmaiden to each and every one of them. It is safe to say that you have to be a certain type of person to understand them properly. It's probably much easier to love a dog or a hamster, because those animals are more predictable, but to love a cat requires you to be completely selfless.

Witches have always had friendly felines as familiars—animal companions—and many people believe them to be psychic. During the Middle Ages in Europe through the seventeenth century, cats were often burned at the stake or drowned along with witches (who might or might not have been their owners) and at times just killed outright. This was because cats were assumed to be witches' familiars—especially black cats. The Egyptians revered cats, but sadly, if a pharaoh died, his special feline would have to join him in the afterlife too. It would be embalmed and placed in the pharaoh's tomb to be ready for the journey to the spiritual realm.

Many people just can't relate to cats. They do not understand why well-fed housecats who go outside seem to kill birds and mice just for the fun of it. There is a reason, though—in order to survive, the cat must keep its hunting skills sharp in case it gets lost or trapped. When your feline friend really loves you, he will hunt for you. Little "gifts" and "offerings" left on the doorstep are meant as a thank-you for your care of him. "Here," they seem to say, "I have caught this for your breakfast . . . enjoy!" Thank him politely for the sweet little offering, then dispose of the poor creature in private so as not to offend your feline. He doesn't realize that you are actually disgusted with the prize-sized rat he just wrestled to the ground in order to feed you!

FAMILIARS

Legend has it that a witch's familiar is a spirit (usually an animal) that supports a witch by aiding her magickal work. In past times, the feline was strongly associated with the witch, and some superstitions even held that a witch would magickally transform herself into a cat. Today, a familiar can be any treasured pet—dog, cat, or bird—that belongs to a witch. She is likely to have a special connection with the pet, and it with her. Those of us who have had the pleasure of having a deep love for a special pet know how important these creatures become in our lives and how we think of them as members of the family.

My familiar is a seal point Siamese cat called Oliver, and he is always present when I am casting my spells. Though he can be a little naughty at times, I think he is attracted to the spiritual energies that flow when a spell is in full swing, and he always stays in the room when any magick is being made.

One year Oliver hit an all-time high and killed fifty-three rats. The residents of our small hamlet were delighted with his efforts and nicknamed him "the Assassin." I think this title went to his head, because the following spring, Oliver tried to bring down a big black cow in a neighboring field and ended up being tossed into the air. Another time Oliver was marauding on the roof and expertly caught a huge seagull by the legs. The gull took off in full flight with my little assassin still hanging on to his feet. I was sitting in bed sipping my morning tea and reading the newspaper, and I watched him fly past the bedroom window at full speed. Thankfully, Oliver finally did let go, landing unceremoniously, and fortunately unhurt, on the patio table.

We Wiccans believe that, like our pets, we emanate love and sincerity, and therefore we have a natural connection with our familiars. I smile when I realize that Oliver took it upon himself to choose me as his witch, so that makes him mine: how lovely! I think I'll swap the seagull for a broomstick, though. . . .

PART THREE

LOVE MAGICK

CHAPTER 10

LEANNA

LOVE
WISDOM

MY PSYCHIC ANTENNAE ARE TWITCHING; I can sense all of you budding witches out there brandishing those wands in magickal anticipation of love and romance! Before we go any further, just hang on for a second. Although there are no hard-and-fast rules with Wicca, the subject of love magick should come with a warning label attached to it. Over the years, I have made plenty of romantic blunders, so I am hoping that this chapter will enable you to bypass most of the common mistakes I have shamelessly made and help you to cast spells for love without any unfortunate consequences.

A LITTLE STORY BEFORE WE BEGIN

He was six foot two, with tousled blond hair, bright blue eyes, and the body of an Adonis—and he didn't even know that I existed! I was twenty-one, and oh, did I love Robert (at least that's what we will call him here). I would watch him standing at the bar every Friday evening, casting his bedroom eyes toward a different woman each week, but he never looked in my direction. No amount of flirting, winking, pouting, or accidentally falling into his lap seemed to work. After three weeks of trying to get his attention, I decided there was only one thing for it. I would get out the old, battered spell book that I had picked up at a tag sale the summer before and *make* him want me. And so, after a tiresome search for lots of strange ingredients (I did have to find a substitute for the unicorn droppings), I set out to cast my spell.

I had never worked with effigies—carved or molded representations of people—before, and am pleased to say I have not created one since. For modern witches, effigies have always been considered to be a little primitive, a little on the dark side, but in this instance, I threw caution to the wind and went ahead, regardless. For the spell, I had to melt down a pink candle with a few other ingredients into a saucepan and then leave it to cool slightly. When it had solidified somewhat but was still pliable, I molded it into the shape of a man, then kissed it three times and buried it in the garden. I

followed the spell to the letter and chanted my words, "*Robert will love me forever,*" over the little mound of soil.

The next week, I wore my cutest outfit and went in search of Robert in the usual spot. It was no surprise when our eyes finally met across that crowded room and he immediately came over and offered to buy me a drink! I was overjoyed that my spell had actually worked, and I gave myself a mental pat on the back. Throughout the evening, Robert attentively brought me glasses of wine, five at least. At the end of the night, feeling rather tipsy, we exchanged phone numbers and agreed to meet the next day.

The Great Goddess above might have blessed the man with astonishingly good looks and a body to die for, but when they were serving out personalities, it's safe to say that poor Robert was at the back of the queue! During our first official date, I tried for two whole hours to make some kind of conversation with him, but he just sat staring at me, inanely grinning. I asked about his job, his hobbies, his family, and, as a last-ditch attempt, even his ex-girlfriends, but each time I asked a question he replied with a one-syllable answer. I wasn't sure whether his nonexistent character traits were somehow the result of my spell casting or whether he just had the personality of a rock. No, I decided, this date wasn't for me. I had made a bad judgment (I was young, after all) and I would just have to let him down gently: pat him on the hand, tell him it had all been very nice, but— oh, look at the time!

I awoke the next morning to find Robert standing outside my house. He had been there all night. He said that he just needed to be near me—he felt so drawn to me. I was his soul mate and he could never live without me! Okay, now it was getting creepy, but at least he had managed to string a few words together. I tried to discourage his attentions by feigning another boyfriend, but even that didn't work. Fourteen bouquets of flowers and six boxes of chocolates later, I decided I had better have a little word with my mother and tell her what I had done. She peered at me sharply over the top of her tiny gold-framed glasses, as she always did, and got out another old, battered spell book to try and fix the problem. So, you see, it's very easy to cast a spell to win someone's heart—but in the end it took three months of my mother's constant spell casting to finally put an end to it!

SOME GUIDELINES FOR
CASTING LOVE SPELLS

Before we venture into casting spells for love, there are some situations we should definitely avoid. As with any Wiccan practice, we should make very certain that our intentions are honorable and that we are not casting spells for our own personal gain. The first important rule—which I learned the hard way with Robert—is: *never cast a love spell to bewitch a certain someone.* If you are crazy about the guy in the office or have a passion for your driving instructor, let nature take its course. If you are meant to be with someone, then you will be. Every relationship that we enter into is spiritually planned (even the bad ones). It's decided before we reincarnate who we are meant to share part, or all, of our lives with. This is because every time we venture into a relationship, we learn something from it. Sometimes, we have to reincarnate with the same husbands and wives in more than one lifetime because one just isn't enough to experience all the things we need to.

If it wasn't our fate to be with our partners, we would never have been at that particular place at that particular time when we had our first meeting. We wouldn't have been attracted to them, for starters, so something must have happened to ignite that spark. No matter how difficult some relationships are, it was fate that brought you together. So when you feel it's time to move away from a relationship, that part of your journey has obviously run its course. Your subconscious is telling you that you can learn nothing more from that partner.

This brings me to the second rule, which is: *never cast a spell to win back an ex-partner.* Witches believe devoutly that everyone has free will, and, as I have mentioned previously, under no circumstances must we meddle with or influence another person's mind. When we exert power over another, we are in fact interfering with that person's karmic lessons. Who knows—maybe Robert was meant to meet the love of his life in those three months he sat pining for me! So, no matter how tempting it is to get the man of your dreams the magickal way, it's really not considered ethical.

However, you are not doing anything wrong when you cast spells to meet new people or to attract love into your life, so let's now look at a few wonderful spells that are tried and tested and safe to use. Those single witches out there who want to spice up their Friday nights can do so with perfect peace of mind. There is also a spell to add a little zing to a marriage. Give them a try, and good luck!

TO ATTRACT A NICE NEW LOVER

Begin on a Friday
Moon Phase—Full

In the evening, take a pink candle and inscribe your name in the wax. Put the candle in a holder and place it in the center of your altar. Take a handful of pink rose petals and scatter these around the base of your candle. Light the candle and say the following incantation nine times:

> I summon Shianna, the angel of love,
> To shine her magick from above.
> Be rid of my solitude,
> No more alone,
> Soul to soul, to make us whole.

After you have said the spell nine times, close the ritual by saying:

So mote it be.

Leave the candle to burn all the way down without disturbing it and then scatter the petals in the garden. You should find love within a few weeks.

IMPROVE YOUR POPULARITY WITH A MAGICKAL MAGNET

Moon Phase—Full

Some people just walk into a room and the guys or girls come flocking. This spell—primarily for women—guarantees that you will never have to dance alone at a party. If you need to increase your popularity when you are out or to give your self-esteem a boost, you can have the men congregating around you with a simple spell.

Before you go out for the evening, take a small drawstring bag and a small magnet of any shape or size and place them on your altar. Light a red candle and place your favorite lipstick next to it. Say this incantation seven times:

This night I will shine, I look divine,
All through the evening
The glamour is mine.

Leave the candle to burn while you are getting ready to go out. Before you leave the house, blow out the candle and place the lipstick and the magnet inside the drawstring bag. Carry the bag in your purse and watch those guys beat a path to your side.

TO ☉ SPICE UP A MARRIAGE

Begin on a Friday
Moon Phase—New

All marriages and long-term relationships go through rough times as well as boring patches. When they do, you can work a little magick to bring back the romance and add a bit of excitement. Draw yourself a bath and add to the water a few drops of lavender oil and a handful of red rose petals. Soak in the water for fifteen minutes or so, then collect some of the bathwater in a jug and discard the petals. Take two empty oyster shells and pour some of the bathwater into one of the shells. Place the other shell over the top and say this incantation three times:

Blessings bestow,
Our romance will grow,
Devoted once more
Just like before,
With a magickal shell
All will be well.

When you have said the spell three times, close it by saying the words:

So mote it be.

Empty the water down the sink, but keep the shells in your bathroom for a week. You can repeat this ritual once a month if you really want to work on your marriage.

EASIER SAID THAN UNDONE

There are witches the world over who bend the rules a little (or a lot!) where affairs of the heart are concerned, but I cannot stress enough how important it is that you work in an appropriate and moral way. So many times I have been asked to reverse a love spell when the inevitable has happened, and as easy as they are to cast, these spells are exceptionally hard to undo.

Shawn's Tip

Remember that everyone's heart and mind belong to them and you have no right to tamper or interfere. So now that you have all the facts, go out there, find a nice partner, and enjoy it for however long it lasts.

HAND-FASTINGS

THE GLITZ AND GLAMOUR OF TODAY'S white weddings actually derive from the ancient pagan betrothal ceremony called the handfasting. The tradition of this hand-clasping ritual is believed to date back to Roman times. It is thought that a handfasted bride and groom initially took their vows only for a year and a day. After that time, if they were still madly in love, another ceremony was held to unite them permanently. In the twenty-first century, Wiccans do still get handfasted, but like most things, handfasting has evolved with the times. Angelic Wiccans tend to have ceremonies based on conventional handfasting, but with services attuned to the vibrations of angels rather than the pagan gods and goddesses.

CEREMONIAL OFFICIANTS

As in the olden days, a high priest or priestess usually performs the handfasting ceremony, either outdoors or in a place of worship, such as a Christian church. Rings are exchanged to symbolize unbroken union and the eternal circle of life. It is interesting to note that the wedding ring, which is traditionally worn on the fourth finger of the left hand, came to be placed there because our ancestors believed that it sat over an artery that ran directly from the hand to the heart.

The high priest or priestess is traditionally clothed in a gothic-style outfit, usually in green, gold, or lavender. These outfits typically include ornate headdresses, and the priestess may wear a crown graced with a variety of crystals and feathers. These high-ranking clergy are mostly mature members of covens who have a wealth of knowledge about spell casting and all things magickal.

THE WITCH'S WEDDING ALTAR

For the ceremony, a lavish full-size altar adorned with a purple cloth is set up outdoors, often near water or a stream. Upon it are placed two large white candles, representing the male and the female, and an elaborately decorated broomstick is propped up at the front. The cake, typically fruitcake, is placed in the center of the altar, along with a chalice of red wine, a plate of biscuits, and a tiny pot of honey. The wine represents a creative union, the biscuits are a symbol to ensure that the couple will never starve, and the honey is to keep the union sweet. Crystals, such as amethyst and rose quartz, are scattered around the table, along with lots of seasonal flowers and petals. The altar can accommodate almost anything the couple chooses, such as photos, trinkets, and personal items, but salt, water, and incense are almost always included. These symbolize the elements and purify the space.

GUESTS, GIFTS, AND POTLUCK

As with non-Wiccan weddings, the number of guests in attendance depends on how many people the couple chooses to invite. Most handfastings are very informal, and they're usually not catered. Guests may be asked to prepare a signature dish, cook an old-fashioned delicacy, or bring a first-rate bottle of wine or a case of imported beer. These days, it is not so fashionable to buy large, expensive gifts or home appliances; most witches feel that small, homemade items or foods are more personal and allow each and every person invited to contribute in some way.

All of these offerings are placed on trestle tables, and once the wedding ceremony is over, the guests help themselves to the many mouth-watering contributions. Witches don't tend to be materialistic, so this potluck arrangement is ideal for us, and it keeps the costs to a minimum. I'm sure you'll agree that this makes the term "the more the merrier" very true indeed.

Sometimes guests are encouraged to dress up in medieval costumes and even allowed to bring along "well-behaved" pets. At my handfasting, six of my chickens escaped from their coop and mingled with the people, which just added to the festive atmosphere.

As guests arrive, gentle music is played in the background and each person is offered a glass of wine. Chairs are placed in a large circle around the altar (which is off-center in the circle), and the guests sit, drink, and await the celebration.

Once all the guests are seated, the "right-hand man" (usually a member of the groom's family or a good friend) walks into the circle, ringing a handbell. This cleanses the area inside the circle of any negative energy. The bride's maid of honor then takes dried lavender flowers mixed with small chips of rose quartz and casts them at the feet of the guests for good luck. At the same time, one of the bride's handmaidens or bridesmaids follows the right-hand man, waving a smudging stick or some sage incense from the altar to further purify the circle.

THE CEREMONY

The service commences with the groom and the high priest or priestess approaching the altar, accompanied by hand drummers. Let's imagine that this ceremony is conducted by a high priestess. The high priestess carries an ornamental cushion with colorful ribbons or cords draped across it. These will be used later to bind the couple's hands in matrimony. If it's a breezy day, the ribbons are pinned to the cushion to keep them in place.

After the groom and the priestess have taken their places at the altar, the drummers return to the bridal party and drum the bride and the handmaidens into the circle. The groom's attire is of his choosing; he may be wearing a frock coat or a fancy, colorful vest. The bride is usually color-coordinated with the groom. She may wear something long and flowing, not necessarily white, accessorized with a headdress or a wreath of seasonal flowers on her head and possibly a wand tipped with rose quartz. The bride has her handmaidens in attendance throughout the service, and there can be as many or as few as she wants. Their costumes are often very witchlike—long, dramatic, gothic-style dresses in rich fabrics such as velvet, with colors ranging from deep purples and reds to vibrant turquoise. Each handmaiden wears a pentagram necklace or ring.

THE SERMON AND VOWS

There are many different types of handfasting services. They can last from around fifteen minutes to a half hour, and the ceremonial texts can vary considerably. Sermons are read and vows are exchanged, as in traditional non-Wiccan weddings; prewritten sermons are available on the Internet to download. In Angelic Wicca, the sermon focuses on angels; archangels are called upon to bless the couple to ensure that they go on to have a happy union together.

Once the bride and groom are standing in front of the altar, the high priestess takes a handful of salt and casts it at their feet. This is said to purify the ground they stand on. She asks the bride and groom to lower their heads, then throws a handful of salt above them to cleanse the air around them. After the high priestess has given her sermon and asked the angels to send eternal blessings, she takes a small silver spoon dipped in honey and gently places it on the lips of the couple to sweeten their life together. A goblet of wine is then offered to each of them, and they drink in turn from the same vessel. The bridesmaids offer baskets to the couple and to all the guests; as the bride and groom each take a bite from theirs, so do their guests, to symbolize sustenance.

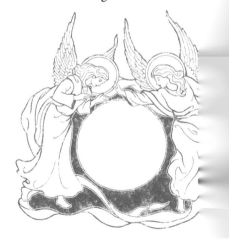

The bride and groom have usually written their personal vows in private and have not shared them with each other beforehand. Many witches like to stand at a lectern and speak their promises to their partner so that all can hear. When the vows have been spoken, the bride and groom exchange rings and the high priestess prepares to bind the couple's hands.

THE BINDING

The handfasting ceremony culminates in hand binding. In the past, couples would have their hands bound together and knotted with cord. Although some witches still like to use cord, many brides and grooms today opt for satin ribbons in purple, green, and white. These are about six and a half feet in length and wound around the bride's and groom's clasped left hands. The expression "tying the knot" likely derives from this ritual.

The high priestess coils the ribbons, weaving them in and out of the couple's fingers before holding their tied hands in the air for a few moments. Ethereal, angelic music plays as the pair begin to walk around the circle, displaying their joined hands and sharing their happiness with everyone. In turn, the guests shower the newlyweds with rice (contrary to popular belief, it s a myth that raw rice will injure birds). In pagan times, rice throwing was believed to transfer the spirit of the fertile grain to the bride and groom, ensuring that they would have a prosperous harvest and a fertile union.

Once this ancient ritual has been completed, the high priestess unties the couple's hands and pronounces them handfasted; the groom then kisses his bride. However, it doesn't end there, because many witches love to follow tradition and jump the broom, which has been propped up against the altar. The drummers bang on their drums as the newlyweds take a running jump over this ornate broom to finalize the marriage. The British phrase "living over the brush" comes directly from this custom; it signifies a couple who have not had an official wedding ceremony but are wed in the eyes of the community. At this point everybody cheers and applauds the newlywed couple and the ceremony is over.

THE CAKE

It has always been customary for the bride and groom to slice a fruitcake, holding the knife together and showing their affection by kissing over the top of it. This is supposed to guarantee that together they will bring forth many children. Then, by sharing the cake with their guests, they are indirectly sharing the magickal energies of their love and passing it on to everyone present. I was terribly lucky, because my maid of honor was a wonderful baker and she made me a beautiful cake in the shape of a pentagram. Afterward, she told me that she had cast a lovely spell over it to make our marriage a happy one.

THE PARTY

This is a wedding reception with a difference. There is no first dance. Instead, live musicians play instruments such as the fiddle, the cello, and the accordion throughout the dinner. After eating and drinking, the guests, in high spirits, start to dance. After a few dances, the groom makes a speech and thanks all of his guests and his right-hand man for their help and assistance.

The bride next makes a thank-you speech and gives small gifts to each of her handmaidens, the high priestess, and her new mother-in-law. This offering is usually in the way of something small and personal, such as a crystal, a magickal pouch, or a fresh bunch of herbs. Right after she has given her presents, she summons all the single people (male and female) for the bouquet toss. Whoever catches this bouquet must take it home and dry it to ensure that they meet their true love in this lifetime.

A WITCHY WEDDING ALBUM

Unlike a non-Wiccan wedding album, which usually holds photographs of the happy couple and their immediate family, a Wiccan wedding album is a more interactive reminder of the couple's special day. Usually, the right-hand man purchases a large hardback book and decorates the outside in some way. Inside, there is a written copy of the sermon and vows from the ceremony. After the ceremony each guest writes a "well wishing" note on the pages that follow, and some of the dried lavender is collected from the ground and pressed into the book. Later, photographs can be added, along with other mementos, such as cards from guests or a copy of the invitation. This treasure is then kept in a special area in the couple's home so that they can maintain all their wonderful memories in one place.

Shawn's Tip

Sadly, a handfasting is not considered legally binding, but witches across the world feel that the ceremonies represent much more than a legal piece of paper. Although handfastings are informal, they are touching and beautiful ceremonies. You may want to have a civil ceremony first and then arrange your handfasting—or "real" wedding, as I have often heard the angelic handfasting called—at a later date. To ensure a magickal marriage, hold your event on or during a New Moon phase, and don't forget the tent, as you cannot guarantee the weather!

PART FOUR

PSYCHIC ABILITY
AND
DIVINATION

SHARPEN YOUR PSYCHIC SKILLS

ANY PEOPLE ASSUME THAT WICCANS are "seers"—that we have the ability to see and sense what others simply cannot, because of our connection to nature, or the devil, or the cosmos, or what have you. (The devil definitely has nothing to do with it as Wiccans do not believe that the devil exists!) The truth of the matter is that we are better able to tune in to what may happen, or what may already be happening where we can't see it, but the reason is simply that we have a deep connection to our intuition. We listen to it, we follow it, we rely on it.

Our prehistoric ancestors depended heavily on their instincts and intuition, which they used to respond to everything from changes in climate to the presence of predators or prey. Over time, many of us in the Western world have lost touch with this ability and come to disregard that part of our internal makeup. But everyone is born with ESP, or extrasensory perception. We all experience gut feelings and hunches; if we only listened to these feelings a little more, we could avoid many of the problems we find ourselves facing on a day-to-day basis. Have you ever met someone for the first time and felt the hair on the back of your neck stand on end? I know I have. Although the person may seem charming enough, your first impression, as incongruous as it may be, can often be right. This is your sixth sense kicking in, and it should never be ignored. Whether you believe it or not, you *are* psychic. Each and every person residing on this planet has some level of psychic ability, whether their psychic "door" is wide open, tightly closed, or left ajar.

If you were raised in a culture where intuitive abilities were encouraged and honed, you'd be in touch with them all of the time, but unfortunately, we Westerners are told from an early age that if you can't see it, it doesn't exist. Any child who claims to see spirits, or who just *knows* things (like a little girl who always says, "Grandma's about to call" just before the phone rings), is dismissed as having an overactive imagination and told to stop exaggerating and "tell the truth!"

The situation is not helped by the hundreds of so-called psychics out there who are quick to con the general public out of a few bucks in order to line their own pockets. Leanna and I are both natural clairvoyants and travel in many different psychic circles, and we have both come up against these professional charlatans who, sadly, give the rest of us a bad name. A genuine mystic can spot a bogus psychic a mile away, but some susceptible folk may not realize they are being conned until it's too late.

Psychic abilities take many forms. The term *ESP* is often used as a catchall phrase to cover everything from heightened intuition to clairvoyance, clairaudience, psychometry, telepathy, dowsing, precognition, scrying, and mediumship. Some of these topics are covered in this chapter; others will be discussed elsewhere in this book. After you have read this chapter, you'll be more aware of your particular psychic abilities. We all have our own strengths and weaknesses, so don't be surprised to learn that some of your abilities are better developed than others.

By now, you're probably thinking, "Hey, I want to start using my ESP! How do I find these gifts?" First, relax. It's going to take a little work to uncover them and get them revved up again!

PSYCHICS THROUGH THE CENTURIES

The term *psychic* comes from the Greek word *psychikos*, meaning "of the soul." In fact, somewhere in your schooling, you probably read or heard about the Delphic oracle, the famed priestess at the Temple of Apollo in Delphi, who would deliver predictions that purportedly came straight from Apollo. Was this telepathy? Clairaudience? We will never know . . . but we do know that the Greeks put a great deal of trust in these revelations and looked to such oracles to deliver news from the future on a regular basis.

However, historical ESP isn't limited to the ancient Greeks. The Bible is filled with prophets warning the masses of things to come. Some people listened, some ignored them, and some became true believers when these visions came to fruition. Joan of Arc can be seen as another example: although Christians view her visions as divine prophecies, she wouldn't have been seeing anything without a heightened state of awareness, which can certainly be categorized as ESP.

There are other famous psychics and seers, some dead, some living: Nostradamus, Edgar Cayce, and John Edward, among others. Although their methods vary, those with fully developed clairvoyant abilities are able to open their minds and tap into psychic energies to see, hear, or know what others seemingly cannot.

PRIME YOUR PSYCHIC PUMP

No one—not even a Wiccan—can just jump into psychic living after years of being shut down. You have to ease into it gently by reminding the right side of your brain of its limitless capabilities. So the first step in finding your ESP is to acknowledge that you have the power to access information that was previously hidden from you. To do this, I suggest you start every day by reminding yourself of this fact. A simple affirmation or mantra will do, something like "My brain is wide open and ready to receive information."

The next thing you should do is to begin researching. Start with metaphysical bookstores, where you'll most likely find not only a wealth of materials, but staff who are eager to share their knowledge and experience with you. This is a good place to ask about nearby Wiccan or psychic groups. The Internet, of course, is another excellent research tool. Google "improve your psychic skills" or "Wicca psychic abilities" and see what pops up.

Learning as much as you can about a given psychic ability, especially one you feel you have an affinity for, will help you understand what you're dealing with and how to get the most out of it. In fact, narrowing down the field of psychic possibilities is a good starting point. Learn your strengths, and understand that most people are extrasensory in only one or two ways.

If you were extrasensory in every way possible, you'd have a terrible time getting through the day on this earthly plane, as you'd be bombarded nonstop with information!

Extrasensory Training

Use these tips for checking in with your mind and assessing its potential:

- Close your eyes, clear your mind, and let your senses guide you. Are you able to "feel" what's in front of you, even though you aren't physically touching it? Can you "see" what's happening in your office, although you aren't there?

- Learn to focus in on the senses even when you're surrounded by distractions. The next time you're on a crowded street, see if you can quiet your mind, isolate each sense, and keep moving, all at the same time. This will train your senses to stay heightened in any situation.

- After a week or two of concentrated sense training, start putting your senses to the test. Begin by making simple predictions. Let's say you're standing in line at the coffee shop. Use your burgeoning power-senses to size up the guy in front of you. What will he order? What will he say to the person serving behind the counter? Will he pay with cash or credit card?

I know the little exercises on the previous page sound simple, but developing ESP begins with redeveloping the senses in this basic way. Most of us go through the day trying to shut out distractions—sounds, smells, and sights that are superfluous to our immediate concerns. In fact, you need to tune back in to all of that. When you do, you'll be amazed at how obvious some things (like the coffee guy's personality and payment habits) start to seem to you—and how easy it is to predict them.

TRUST YOUR INTUITION

Once you start tuning in to your senses on a regular basis, you'll be able to rely on your intuition to guide you through any situation. There are some people who tell me, "My intuition is always wrong! I should just do the opposite of my gut feeling!" These people aren't lacking in intuition; they simply need more practice in sensory training. I suspect they made a poor decision once or twice (probably by going against their gut feeling) and now they're just flummoxed whenever they have an important choice to make. Their senses are in confusion, and their decision-making process is the psychic equivalent of throwing a dart at a board while blindfolded. What do I say to these people? "Take off the blindfold already!" Yes, it really *is* that simple.

So let's say you are one of these people whose intuition is all twisted up in reason and logic and "what-ifs." How can you clear out the cobwebs and get back to acknowledging and trusting your instincts?

1. Start with a simple decision, something like "Should I drive down Main Street or South Street on my way to work today?"
2. One answer will pop into your mind. Make a note of it. That's your

gut feeling. Don't think about it, don't look for logical reasons, don't argue with yourself.

3. Breathe in and out, deeply and quietly, and just let that answer sit. Be confident in your decision to trust your intuition. Push all waffling feelings aside.

4. Now do it. Take the street your intuition chose. Don't be disappointed if your drive goes less than smoothly. If you encounter problems on your way to work (traffic, construction, whatever), that doesn't necessarily mean your intuition was wrong; it could mean that you avoided an accident on the other route—one that didn't happen since you weren't there. So don't throw your hands up and say, "I chose wrong *again*! My intuition is good for nothing!" It's nice when we have a solid positive outcome to hang the intuitive hat on, but we can't always see or know what *didn't* happen because of the choice we made.

Then again, sometimes it's obvious that we've made the wrong decision, like trusting the wrong person, buying the wrong house, or taking the wrong job. If you took the time to check in with your intuition and you think it steered you wrong, let's take a look at your process. Did you ask:

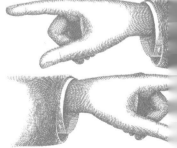

* "Should I date this person?"
* "Should I buy this house?"
* "Should I take this job?"

If so, you may need to get more specific the next time around. There are always lessons—good or bad—to be learned in any life situation, so when you ask if you "should" do something, the answer could easily be, "Hey, why not?" But to learn whether something will bring you more happiness than sorrow, you could ask:

* "Is this person honest and loyal?"
* "Will I be happy living here?"
* "Will I grow and prosper in this job?"

Try this rephrasing process and go with the first answer that pops into your mind. And trust yourself. You know more than you think you do!

LIGHT UP YOUR INTUITION

Here's a simple visualization exercise to get your intuition moving. First, clear your mind of the distractions you've been dealing with all day long. Take the phone off the hook and give the dog a bone to keep him occupied for the next fifteen minutes.

Next, make a list of questions you need answers to—anything from "Is this stock a sound investment?" to "Is my health going to improve soon?" Tailor your questions to your concerns. You'll use this list a bit later in the exercise.

Now close your eyes. Breathe deeply but keep your mind clear—you're not focusing on or analyzing anything, just clearing out the psychic clutter. Imagine a traffic light just as it would appear in real life—red at the top, yellow in the middle, green at the bottom. Start warming up your instincts by asking practice questions. For example, ask, "Is my hair blond?" and see what color lights up in your mind. You should use the three traffic light colors that you envision as your answers: Red is no. Green is yes. Yellow indicates maybe or uncertainty. Ask some other questions you know the answers to, such as:

* "Am I a woman?"
* "Is it Saturday?"
* "Is it the year 2045?"

These kinds of questions will give you a base reading to go on. Ask a question that will give you a "maybe" response, too, since that's always a possible answer.

At this point you're ready to get down to your main concerns. Don't think—just ask. What color appears? That's your answer, and that's all there is to it!

BODY LANGUAGE

Your body's reaction is an integral part of your intuition, so start listening to what it's telling you. Sometimes we want something so much that we avoid obvious signals. If you've recently made a decision and you feel anxious and jittery, don't write that off as nervous excitement. It could be that your body is reacting to what it knows is a bad choice, desperately trying to warn you. On the other hand, a feeling of peace or a surge in positive energy could indicate that you *are* following your intuition and your physical systems are feeling serene as a result. If anxiety is driving you mad over a decision you've made, try clearing your mind and using the traffic-light method just discussed to see if you're really on the right track or if you're headed for an unfortunate detour.

DREAMING OF BETTER INTUITION?

Your dreams are one of the best indicators of your intuition. This is because when you dream, you are using your subconscious mind instead of your conscious mind, which is often cluttered with alternative plans, fears about the future, and that pesky thing called logic.

It's easy to be confused by dreams, though, since a lot of intuitive information comes through in the form of symbols that can seem bizarre to the untrained interpreter. Chapter 15, on dreams, will give you an overview of how to decode your overnight happenings, and you can always go online for help interpreting any symbols not listed there.

Start keeping a dream journal to help you follow what your mind is telling you, especially if you're going through an especially troubling or difficult time. Your mind *wants* to give you the advice you need! Take it, follow it, and rest easy.

STOP ANALYZING!

The most important thing about trusting your instinct is to just go with it. This can be an incredibly difficult task for people who need to analyze every thought they have and every move they make. While there's something to be said for planning and organizing the long-term aspects of your life, there are many things that are out of your control. Life is going to do what it's going to do, and you just have to roll with it sometimes.

For instance, if you're using your intuition to figure out whether or not you should buy a specific house, and it's a house that you really, really want—

and your intuition is saying, "This is not the place for you!"—then you have to be willing to accept that. Don't try to figure out why your mind is working against your wants, just trust that there's a reason. When you rely on your intuition, you'll never be sorry. Your inner compass is not making up new directions for you to follow, it is just steering you down the path you already know you should be on.

TOUCH ME, FEEL ME, READ ME

Psychometry is one form of ESP that some Wiccans use, and one that many people find especially intriguing. It's the ability to hold an object that belongs to someone else and get a "read" on that person. In chapter 18, on remote viewing and clairvoyance, I talk about psychics helping to solve crimes. In such cases, we'll often be asked to hold something that belongs to a missing person or a suspect in the hope that we'll pick up a sensation or emotion that will be helpful in the investigation.

It's quite possible that you've experienced psychometry yourself without realizing it.

Have you ever worn a piece of vintage clothing or jewelry and felt anxious or just "off" somehow? It wasn't because the crinoline was scratching you or the diamond was blinding you; it was probably because the person who wore it before you had the same sense of nervousness. Cloth and metal are "absorbent" elements; clothes and jewelry act like psychic sponges and can soak up vibrations from their wearers. These vibrations—happy or unhappy energies, depending on the owner—often hang around for centuries, so antique objects especially are pervaded with them.

Now, I know this might send you heading for the hills, but the vibrations can be especially strong if the clothing or jewelry was worn by someone who

was dying (or who actually died) while wearing it. This is true only if the person was not at peace about passing to the next plane, though. Clothing and accessories that come from people who are ready to move on are usually cloaked in a sense of serenity and peace.

You can also use psychometry to get a good first impression of a person. Have you ever read the Stephen King book *The Dead Zone*, which was also made into a film and later a television show? The main character, Johnny Smith, has the ability to touch people and see their future. For him, this usually involves a vision of a fiery death, a nuclear war, or involvement in a heinous crime—but don't let that turn you off. It's far more common to use psychometry to get a general feel for someone or for your surroundings than to visualize a dramatic disaster.

So how do you put this psychic sense to work?

1. Practice with a friend. When you meet up for lunch or a shopping date, ask her not to tell you anything about how her day has gone so far, then take her hand as though you're going to shake it. Close your eyes and focus on the energy you're picking up.
2. Let your senses really speak to you. Are you picking up a chill? Does your head suddenly ache? Are you feeling warm suddenly?
3. Interpret these feelings. For example, is it possible your friend just got over a bout of the flu? Remember that feelings don't have to be literal, although you certainly could receive something pretty straightforward. You might also receive a vague sense of general discomfort, which is harder to interpret but definitely gives you an idea of what may be going on with your friend.

As you hone this skill, you can use it to help you gain insight during business dealings and personal interactions. Simply shaking hands with a colleague or associate can give you a heads-up as to what the other person is all about! Find out if your neighbor is on the up-and-up. Know with one (innocent) touch if your blind date is worth your trouble. You can do all this with one hand tied behind your back—you just need the other hand free to do some investigating.

BRAIN TELEGRAMS AND TELEPATHIC MESSAGES

Fans of the *Star Wars* movies know that the Jedi had some serious mind skills going on, namely, in the form of telepathy—sending and receiving thought waves. Some people call this reading minds, others call it communicating without speaking. Whatever you call it, telepathy is awfully convenient, especially if you're in a crowded room and you don't feel like shouting.

We've all had our telepathic moments. Maybe you've been talking with a friend and known exactly what she was going to say before she opened her mouth, or maybe you've both said the same thing at the same time. This is the result of being on the same thought wavelength. As you already know, this is easily achieved with some people (your best friends or loved ones, for example), but not so easily with others (your standoffish boss).

Since you can use telepathy to your advantage, especially in the case of a boss or coworker you just can't relate to, it is an important skill to have in your psychic toolbox. To learn to send and receive telepathic messages, you're going to need a willing and open-minded friend, preferably one you've shared mind waves with in the past. Once you get the hang of using brainwaves, you'll be able to work on your own. For now, get together with that friend and follow these steps:

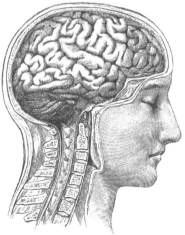

1. Relax. Regular meditation and visualization (discussed later in this chapter and in other chapters) are absolutely essential to warming up your telepathic tendencies. There are parts of your brain that need to be open to the possibilities that surround

you; if they're closed, you can forget about picking up or sending messages through the ether.

So before you begin, allow time for you and your lovely assistant to sit back and chill your minds for ten or fifteen minutes.

2. Decide which of you will be the sender and which will be the receiver. For the sake of this discussion, you're going to be the sender.

3. When you're both relaxed, visualize an image that you want to send. Let's say you're transmitting the thought of a basketball. Really make it real in your mind: the perfect roundness, the knobby, rubbery material, even the smell. It's best to start with an image instead of a thought, because an image is one compact package that isn't subject to getting lost in translation, the way a phrase might be. When you perfect your skill, you'll be able to send and receive thoughts as well.

4. Picture a tube running between your brain and your friend's. Now, send that basketball down the tube. Hold the picture of the ball clearly and steadily in your mind as your friend retrieves the image.

This technique takes practice to perfect. Even though you and your pal might be of like mind, you haven't been purposely accessing these parts of your minds up to this point. So be patient, pour one glass of wine if you like, and have fun with it! (Drinking more than one glass can dull your senses.)

Once you really get the hang of telegraphing with the mind, put it to use when you need it most: in your yearly review at work (send the message "I'm a great worker, and you need to pay me more!"); on a hot date (try "Notice how beautiful and smart I am!"); or even when you take your car in for service (something along the lines of "You are going to be honest and not overcharge me for this work!"). Try to put it to use in as many everyday situations as you can and just wait for the benefits to come back to you. Keep in mind, though, that negative or dishonest thoughts should never be telegraphed—this can invite negative energy and create bad karma.

OPENING THE DOOR TO SUPER PSYCHIC SKILLS

So far, we've been talking about using intuition to help make decisions. This is the first step in bringing your psychic skills to the forefront of your mind, where they belong. Once you're a pro at using your perceptions to assess the world around you, you can start using those same skills to predict what's going to happen. I'm not talking about making yes-or-no decisions in your daily life now, I'm talking about using insight to see what the universe holds in store for you.

At this point I can hear you all saying (and not just because I am a psychic!) "Oh, come on—if I could predict the future, I would be rich, and nothing bad would ever happen to me or my family!" If only psychic powers worked that way. After reading chapter 1 on reincarnation, you know that we are all put into our lives to learn various lessons—and maybe this is just not your time to lead a perfectly charmed life. Wiccans know that there's a definite push and pull in the cosmos, and we're just not meant to see everything before it happens, perhaps especially moments that are meant to teach us something. So don't expect to be receiving all the answers to that important exam you have coming up!

All that said, very skilled psychics can and do see the future. I can let you in on some of the secrets of accessing this skill right here and now.

Using your intuition is a necessary step in becoming psychic, and this largely involves sitting back and listening to what your instincts are telling you. But ESP depends on flexing a little mental muscle too. This may sound contradictory, but what I'm telling you is that you need to regularly *work* the right side of your brain—the side that's responsible for creativity and intuition and that's receptive to psychic messages. It's just like getting stronger anywhere else in your body. If you never lift anything heavier than a can of tuna, you can't expect to have bulging biceps. If you ride in a car all day long, your quadriceps are going to turn to jelly. And if you never work out the creative and visual parts of your brain, they're not going to spit out information when you need it most. So consider me your psychic trainer and allow me to walk you through your first workout.

MEDITATION MANEUVERS

I can't tell you how important it is to take the time to quiet your mind and focus on absolutely nothing. I know it sounds like a luxury, but when you do this, your mind actually opens up to the very things we're talking about—the things you can't see but can only sense. When you learn to put yourself in a deep state of meditation, so many things become crystal clear. We talk about meditation elsewhere in the book, but it's always attached to another process or activity. Here, I'm going to give you all you need to know about meditation for its own sake, step by step:

1. Make sure you are not so exhausted that you end up falling asleep. Meditation involves placing yourself in between the sleeping and waking worlds—you don't want to slip over the edge into pure snoozing.
2. Find a quiet spot without distractions. Make sure the temperature is comfortable and you have a comfortable place to sit or lie down.
3. Light some candles, draw the curtains, and play some quiet music. Binaural tunes, which are recorded in a special way and can induce

relaxing brainwaves, are particularly helpful for drawing you into a meditative state. You can easily download this type of music online.

4. Lie down or sit on the floor or in a chair. Some people like to meditate cross-legged or in the lotus position, others like to keep their feet flat on the floor. I say, assume any position you'll be comfortable in for fifteen to twenty minutes. (If you aren't a yogi, that probably means the lotus position is out.)

5. Close your eyes. Focus on one sound—the ticking of the clock, the whir of a fan, the binaural music, the hum of the furnace. Breathe deeply—in through your nose, out through your mouth.

6. Acknowledge any thoughts that come into your head and picture putting them in a box for later access. Right now, it's quiet time in the brain.

7. Now just relax in the nothingness for as long as you can.

That's really all there is to meditation. It sounds so easy—like, who can't shut off their brain?—but you'd be surprised at how difficult it can be. It's perfectly understandable; we all lead such busy lives, chock-full of appointments, responsibilities, and activities, that it can be tricky to find that quiet place in the mind where the spirit reigns supreme. But that's exactly why we need to do it—so that we don't lose that sense of self.

What does meditation have to do with becoming psychic? Most people's brains are so cluttered with day-to-day *stuff* that they can't see the forest for the trees, so to speak. I knew a woman who worked right next to a guy who was absolutely smitten with her. This was obvious to everyone around her, yet she complained that she was invisible to men! She was so harried with work and her outside activities that she couldn't see what was right in front of her. Because of her brain's cluttered condition, there

was no way she could have accessed her psychic powers if she needed them. Do I think five to ten minutes of meditation a few times each week could have helped her sort out her love life? I sure do. It would have put her in touch with her intuition, with the world around her, and opened up all kinds of "wormholes" for her to travel down where she could engage her powers of prediction.

SEE WHAT YOUR IMAGINATION CAN DO

Even though I'm talking to you about predicting actual events, becoming psychic requires awakening your powers of imagination and visualization as well. This activity is slightly different from meditating, where you want to shut out everything and just *be*. But visualization and imagination exercises start out like meditative workouts, and they go hand in hand.

Find a quiet spot, get into a comfortable position, and close your eyes, just as you would do to begin meditating. This time, though, bring something—an event, a worry, a desire—into your thoughts. Play around with the images, taking them wherever you want. You're controlling the story right now; you can try on different surroundings, different characters, different endings.

You may be asking yourself why you should have to go through all this effort to practice your visualization and imagination, rather than concentrating purely on prediction. Even if your sole aim is prediction (covered in the next chapter), learning to predict events draws on the same part of your brain that holds the imagination, so learning to access and use this region of the mind for visualization strengthens the predictive muscle as well.

Don't Be a Doubter

Maybe one of the most important aspects of becoming and remaining psychic is to simply *believe* in your abilities. When you waffle, stammer, or constantly second-guess yourself, no vision can come out of such self-doubt. Almost immediately, you will begin to toss your intuition out the window, make poor choices, and lose your faith in the whole process. This is exactly why most people believe they are *not* psychic!

So take some advice from a woman who sees and hears the future: the information is out there, and much of it is yours for the asking (and some of it will come to you even when you don't ask). Accept these gifts as they come to you, use them to do good if and when you can, and learn to enjoy the benefits of experiencing life on as many planes as possible.

CHAPTER 13

SHAWN

GAZE INTO THE FUTURE

ALL INTUITIVE PEOPLE HAVE THEIR strengths and weaknesses. Some are clairvoyant, some are scryers. Clairvoyants and scryers tap into the same universal vibrations. It doesn't matter what method you use because the outcome will be the same. If you are a champion image-decipherer (who may say, "Oh, see how that cloud looks like a tree!" or "Wow, that smudge looks like a claw!"), then scrying—also known as crystal gazing, crystal seeing, or simply peeping—might be *your* thing.

The image of a wizened old hag slumped over a crystal ball, gazing into the future, is a rather unfortunate visual associated with witches and scrying. While modern-day witches still use a crystal ball for scrying, today's witches are a new breed. We have access to Botox and other "magickal" potions that keep us young and beautiful, so while the typical appearance of a witch has (we hope) changed, what hasn't altered over time is that most white witches, including yours truly, always have a crystal ball somewhere nearby.

These wonderful objects are not just any old lumps of crystal; they are carefully crafted from the finest materials found on our planet. They are generally clear in appearance, and their size varies from ball to ball: the smallest can fit right into your pocket, whereas the largest orbs are as big as basketballs. Whatever their size, crystal balls are typically mounted on a stand so they don't roll away. A small pillow or pad will do, although some balls come with their own little stands. You should cleanse your crystal ball once a month, either by gently washing it in salt water or by leaving it out under a full moon for the night.

THE SKINNY ON SCRYING

Scrying is a way of "seeing" spiritual visions and foretelling the future by looking into a reflective or mutable surface of some kind. Most scryers use a crystal ball or a bowl of water to conjure up their visions, but others use mirrors, crystals, reflective or luminescent stones, or even smoke and fire. It is said that an expert can see visions in something as small and seemingly insignificant as a thumbnail!

Psychic gazing has been a popular practice for centuries, although for different reasons. Some societies used scrying as a means to connect with God, while others understood these visions to be a link to the universe at large. In any event, scrying has survived the test of time and is still practiced today, although it's generally not highly respected among experts in spiritual or scientific fields.

I think that scrying is such an individual gift, it's impossible to understand or appreciate it unless you can actually *do* it—and if you think you can't scry, then think again. Recent sensory-deprivation studies have given us some insight into how and why visions appear, suggesting that scryers basically shut out distractions from the outside world, allowing their psychic eye to see what no one else sees. In these ganzfeld (German for "complete field" or "full field") experiments, participants were deprived of sound and light for a predetermined amount of time. Afterward, participants reported what, if anything, they saw. Months later, many were surprised to discover that their visions had been portents of things to come. The theory is that by blocking out the physical senses, you allow yourself to access areas of the mind that are, too often, ignored and silenced.

Ganzfeld experiments amount to putting yourself into a trance, and you can try this at home without the bells and whistles of a laboratory setting, although you will need a quiet space. Turn off the TV and radio. Put the dog outside. If your apartment or house is subject to the constant din of motorcycles, sirens, and overhead air traffic, turn on a fan for white noise. Now sit comfortably—on the bed, on a chair, at your kitchen table, on the floor, wherever you choose. Choose one spot on the wall in front of you and stare at it. Let your vision go blurry if you want. Breathe deeply and continue to focus on that one spot. Within a couple of minutes, the spot will begin to darken, suggesting that your sense of sight has had enough. You can continue on at this point—what can you "see" in your mind's eye?—or simply move your eyes to another area of the room to bring yourself, and your senses, back.

I SEE THE HISTORY OF SCRYING

In ancient Egypt, priests and priestesses used scrying as a way to divine the future. They would pour oil or water into a dark vessel and wait for images to appear, using the results to predict the outcome of war, the best time to plant crops, or the best time to conceive a child. The images would be dark and fuzzy, but that didn't really matter. It was their *interpretation* of the images that was important.

As the centuries rolled on, the art of scrying evolved. Some people used scrying as a form of meditation to get in touch with their spiritual sides. Other seers gazed at reflective objects and, perhaps because of the changes in the alpha waves in their brains, were able to enter into hypnotic states, or self-induced trances, in which they predicted future events.

Some scholars believe that Nostradamus, the famous sixteenth-century French psychic, used scrying as a method of divination. It is said that he would often stare into a bowl of water to bring on this special state of consciousness when writing his famous quatrains predicting future wars, deaths, and world calamities.

It wasn't until the Victorian age that the Roma Gypsies, with their dark, flowing hair, gold jewelry, and vibrant sense of style and dress, brought attention back to the crystal ball. The Gypsies were well versed in this divinatory art and charged often hefty fees to anyone who wanted their fortune read. Though Gypsies were much maligned during this period, they were also known to be very good at scrying. In fact, the Gypsies elevated this mystical science to an art form. Their fortune-telling abilities were so revered that when people living in towns and cities saw the wagons coming, they scraped some money together and scurried to have their fortunes read before the Gypsies hit the road again!

CRYSTAL ENHANCEMENT

In those Victorian times, witches, warlocks, and wizards began taking this ancient form of crystal gazing to an even higher level of development and skill. They refined the technique of scrying by choosing crystals with specific properties attached to them and using those crystals for divination, healing, and enlightenment. If a client had a fertility problem, for example, she would hold a crystal or crystals in her hand— usually moonstone and/or rose quartz—while the witch gazed into the scrying surface. The crystal would wipe out the negative forces surrounding the person, opening the door to peace and contentment.

Lapis lazuli was, and still is, often used to help people find inner peace, while rose quartz brought love and self-healing. There are so many stones out there it could boggle the mind, so use the simple list opposite as a starting guide (and see chapter 8, "Crystal Power," for more information on crystals).

To boost the power of the vision, choose a crystal that relates to the reason you're scrying.

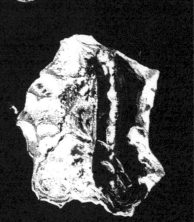

AMETHYST: Higher consciousness
BLUE AGATE: Inner consciousness
CITRINE: Money and success
HEMATITE: Opportunity
QUARTZ: Clarity of mind
SAPPHIRE: Truth
MALACHITE: Past lives

CONNECTING WITH THE CRYSTAL BALL

If you want to give a crystal ball a whirl, try to stop in at a New Age shop. You can buy a crystal ball on the Internet, too, but because I believe that you have to be drawn to a crystal, I really recommend that you try to purchase one in person so you can choose the one that "speaks" or "calls" to you. It's a lot easier to determine a good match if you can pick it up, hold it, feel its vibrations, and connect with it. Stand back, look at the array of balls available in the shop, and see what looks appealing to you. A certain color? A specific material? Hold each ball that you like and just close your eyes for a moment. Does the ball have an energy that you can feel? Does the weight feel right to you? Are you happy holding it?

Some balls have imperfections—smudges, flecks, or bubbles inside the crystal—while others are perfectly clear. Imperfections are not necessarily a bad thing; in fact, they may well help you with your visions. Again, this is a purely personal matter. Some scryers can live with a couple of tiny flaws and others are distracted by them, so you should go with what feels right to you.

RELEASE YOUR MIND AND READ

As with other witchy tools, you should get to know your crystal ball in the privacy of your own home. Begin your first session by creating a soothing, calming environment. Put on some music if that helps. Dim the lights.

Place your ball on its stand or pillow on a table. Light a white candle and place it near the ball. Sit in a comfortable chair, close your eyes, and meditate for a moment. Focus on removing distractions from your mind. I call this a sort of *un*-focusing, allowing yourself to slip into an almost dreamy state of mind. Breathe deeply.

Open your eyes now and look into your ball, but keep that unfocused state going. To see the future, you don't have to ask anything. You may see a cloud taking shape in the ball; you may see visions. You're not trying to see anything specific, so just accept whatever it is that appears and don't try to rush it. Another version of scrying involves asking a question of the crystal ball and then inferring the answer from what you see. We will look at how to interpret your visions a little later.

Crystal-ball purists believe that visions appear in the light of the full moon, though I know scryers who read the ball whenever the mood strikes them. And what do I say? I remind you that *all* these methods are subject to modification, so you should do whatever you find works best for you.

IT'S MY TV AND I'LL SCRY IF I WANT TO

Not long ago, I was sitting daydreaming and my eyes inadvertently drifted over toward my television, which was turned off at the time. I began to see the same kinds of visions on the blank screen that I usually see in my crystal ball. This probably happened because I was in an almost trancelike state and my mind was clear of distractions. Later, I decided to experiment: I turned the television on, but instead of setting it to a particular channel, I simply unscrewed the cable connector and turned the TV to a blank screen with white noise and "snow." White noise is commonly used to connect with ghosts and spirits who are looking to communicate with the living, so I got to thinking, "Why not use it in scrying? Maybe someone out there has something to share with me through white noise." And you know what? I was amazed at the results! In some respects, the visions I encountered were much clearer than the methods of scrying I had tried in the past.

Since you may not have a crystal ball, this method is a great way to try out the skill of scrying without investing in an expensive tool. This is a brand-new divinatory art called "plasma scrying." It's quite simple, and you don't have to pay the cable company for an extra channel on your television set. It's free, courtesy of the Twilight Zone!

The first step in successful plasma scrying is to make sure your television set is either turned off or set to a blank channel. Do not clean the screen. Any smudges or specks will add to your visions, not detract from them. The next important steps are:

1. Do not shut off all the lights in the room or you won't be able to see any reflection on the television screen. In addition to whatever lighting you have in the room, you will also need a white candle. I like to use a small white candle in a glass.

2. Start by saying this prayer: *"To the technology born, I give it light, to show me the way, to my own inner light. So mote it be."* Write this down in your Book of Shadows for future reference.

3. Now, light the white candle and place it in front of the television set. Make sure the candlelight casts a flickering glow or light on the screen.

4. Stare at the blank television screen and begin daydreaming.

5. In your mind, ask the television set a question about anything that is important to you: partner, job, career, or family. Within about ten minutes the answer should be revealed.

Reading the Results

Remember when you were a kid gazing at the clouds in the sky and you swore they looked liked dragons, or faces, or rocket ships, or other imaginary shapes in your mind? Some of the images were scary, some were comforting, others were just there. I want you to use that same skill to associate an image with the flickering lights on the television screen. Does the image look dark and scary or happy or warm? What feelings do you get from the image?

This is where a trancelike state of mind comes into play. To interpret what you're seeing, you have to get off the mental plane and into a zoned-out state where those images can come to life. People sometimes ask me how to "read" what they're seeing, as though there are right, wrong, or definite answers in the world of scrying. Whatever you see will be related to your own experiences or, if you're reading for someone else, connected to something happening in that person's life. Let's say you conjure up a vision of a flute—and your grandmother happened to be a flutist. Perhaps the message coming through is from her or about her. If a vision is difficult to see or appears to be very small, it probably means that it's either a past event or something that will happen in the distant future. Strong, clear visions indicate something that is imminent.

Colors in your visions can also indicate what's to come:

WHITE: Protection, positive energy

RED: Danger

ORANGE: Anger

YELLOW: Trouble, obstacles ahead

BLUE: Success

GREEN: Happiness, health

BLACK, GRAY: Negative energy

What if nothing happens—nada—and you're just sitting there staring at an empty screen for ten minutes? Read on to find out.

Smaller Scryers

If the TV screen came up empty for you or you are not near a TV, take out your laptop computer and open it, but don't turn it on. Place it on your lap. Repeat all the above steps, but omit the lit candle to avoid setting yourself or your computer on fire.

If nothing has worked for you thus far, take out your smart phone or any mobile-technology toy. Stare at the reflection on the screen for five minutes. (Again, forget lighting a candle. You have enough problems at the moment trying to conjure up an image.) I'll bet my witch's cap you will see something. Why? It's like learning anything else. Sometimes, to see, you have to start small, and a tiny screen can help you focus more quickly and more clearly.

The Secret Revealed

Some people think that when they stare at their blank TV, they will see a live television show of the future. That's not really what we're trying to do, but if this exercise inspires you to write a script or a proposal, then by all means, go for it.

Successful scrying isn't like watching a show; it's all in the interpretation of the dust spots, smudges, fingerprints, and reflections of light on the screen. It is up to you to mentally process those shapes and forms and discover how they relate to you. This is the same principle as cloud-watching and can be applied anytime, anywhere.

Each person has their own divinatory ability that is unique only to them. But in order to succeed at this art, you have to try each and every one of the methods to find the one that you are most comfortable with and enjoy the most.

Leanna's Tip

I am not the best scryer in the world, but I do have a crystal ball that I treasure. Because crystals are "alive"—each one coming from the earth and having its own unique energy field—I thought it was a nice touch to actually give my ball a name, and so I called him Clifford. Clifford sits proudly in the corner of my room on an ornate stand. I always cover Clifford with a purple cloth when he is not in use. This not only keeps the ball clean, dust-free, and ready to engage with at any time, it also entraps all its energy and power beneath the most spiritual color of all.

CHAPTER 14

SHAWN

COUNT ON THE NUMBERS

SOME PEOPLE SEE NUMBERS AND THEY immediately get nervous. They sweat, they tremble, and suddenly they're back in tenth-grade math class with their heads swirling, not grasping a single concept!

If this describes you, it would be perfectly understandable for you to avoid the field of numerology. However, it would also be unfortunate, since numerology is one of the easiest forms of divination to master. In fact, many Wiccans, including me, believe in a mystical "name-over" that involves changing your name and, by doing so, changing your destiny to reach a more spiritual path in life (more about that later when I talk about your destiny number). I promise there are no complex formulas to calculate, no theorems to wrap your head around, and no written tests.

How easy is this numbers game? With a person's name and birth date, you can unlock a wealth of information about them.

PYTHAGOREAN PASSION

Numerology has been around for a long time. Pythagoras, the famous ancient Greek mathematician, refined the system used today sometime around the sixth century BCE. Although little is known about Pythagoras, it is believed that he and his followers considered numbers and divination to be universally interconnected.

By using the alphabet as a guide, the Pythagorean system of numerology assigns meaning to numbers in order to predict the future and intuit information about a person's character.

According to legend, while Pythagoras was alive, there were those who believed that his theories were dangerous and others who dismissed his writing as the ramblings of a madman. Because of this, he swore his many students to secrecy. Eventually, intimidated by his critics, Pythagoras set sail for Egypt, where he studied with the Chaldeans and developed his numerological theories

further before moving on to Italy to set up his own school of philosophy. It is believed that this is where his true brilliance in mathematics emerged, giving rise to his theories in geometry, which are still taught in schools around the world today.

CALLED TO CALCULATE

Like Pythagoras, when I sat in class in the seventh grade, I saw numbers in a totally different light. To me, they were vibrant and alive and jumped and danced across the blackboard. It was as if the numbers were speaking to me, and each digit had its own secret story to tell.

I probably had the only seventh-grade math teacher who assigned a project requiring further research in the local library. I call that fate, for reasons that will become clear in a moment. Bundled up in my warmest clothes, I trudged two miles in a heavy snowstorm, silently wishing that I were out with my mates, tossing snowballs. Instead, I was headed to sit for hours in sterile surroundings, reading books on mathematical theories.

When I walked into that imposing building, I headed straight to the librarian and asked her if she had any books on numbers. Maybe she saw something in my eyes that set me apart from the other kids who passed through those massive oak doors, or maybe she was psychic and saw something within me that led her to believe I was seeking a much deeper truth. I'll never know, but I recall her handing me an old, tattered book on numerology, which I took over to a desk to read. When I opened the book and looked inside, chills ran up and down my spine. The pages were filled with information about a discipline that was completely foreign to me, where numbers had personalities and vibrations!

I can't remember how long I sat at that long wooden desk devouring the information, but what I do know is that my life changed forever on that fateful snowy day. I was about to embark upon a journey that would lead me into the strange and mysterious world of numerology.

NAMES, NUMBERS, AND PERSONALITY

The ancient teachings of numerology tell us that a name is more than just a collection of letters. These letters hold the key to your future and your destiny, and they affect how others perceive you. It's very easy to unlock the secrets of this art. To begin with, you need just two vital pieces of information—your name and your birth date.

At its simplest, nine numbers are used to set up a numerology chart: 1, 2, 3, 4, 5, 6, 7, 8, and 9. Each of the letters in a person's name corresponds to a number that you can easily find in the chart below.

1	2	3	4	5	6	7	8	9
A	B	C	D	E	F	G	H	I
J	K	L	M	N	O	P	Q	R
S	T	U	V	W	X	Y	Z	

Let's suppose your name is SUSAN DOE. You find your name number by adding together all the numbers that correspond to the letters in your name until you reach a number from 1 to 9. Let's see what Susan Doe's name number comes out to be, using the chart.

S=1, U=3, S=1, A=1, N=5, D=4, O=6, E=5
1 + 3 + 1 + 1 + 5 + 4 + 6 + 5 = 26.

Now we reduce 26 to a single digit by adding the digits together:
2 + 6 = 8. Susan Doe's name now translates to a number 8, which denotes someone who possesses visionary powers and is highly intuitive.

Try this with your own name and see what your number says about your personality. The complete breakdown of numbers and their meanings is in the next section.

YOUR PERSONALITY NUMBER

1: The Teacher

If your name number adds up to one, you are compassionate and sincere. You may feel the pain of others and want to reach out and help. You are not afraid of challenges and you're excellent at solving problems. Friends come to you with their troubles, seeking guidance and help. You are a deep thinker who teaches by example, so expect to spend a lot of time deep in thought. There is an imaginative and bright side to your nature, making you able to achieve anything you set your mind to.

On the negative side, you can be either extremely bossy or awfully shy, so try and find a balance somewhere in between. You may also have a tendency to leap before you look, so slow down and try not to be so impulsive.

2: The Nurturer

Twos see the best in everyone and are very tolerant when dealing with people's faults. You may feel that you have a kinship with those less fortunate than yourself, so you try to lift people's spirits by offering hope and optimism. Having two as your personal number means that you are wise, understanding, and sensitive. You have a harmonious aura that makes your personality magnetic. You are altruistic and nurturing, and you have leadership qualities that allow others to feed off your positivity.

At times you tend to hold back and not stick up for yourself. The lesson here is to try and become more assertive.

3: The Wise One

Threes are the first people friends and loved ones turn to for advice. Threes' innate wisdom is always dependable, always available. When presented with life's problems or challenges, you don't run a mile in the opposite direction; rather, you face them head on. Animals and nature play an important part in your life, and you will undoubtedly have a pet or two at some stage. You are charismatic, charming, positive, and determined. You are also gentle and wise beyond your years and have the ability to make everyone feel good.

Self-indulgence could be a problem, especially if you like your food and creature comforts. You also hate vigorous routine, so a monotonous job is not for you. Instead, you prefer a career that is changeable and imaginative.

4: The Seeker

Fours are quick wits! You have a tendency to look at everything under a finely tuned microscope and to be extremely analytical of others. Your earnest desire is to explore life and seek alternative roads to travel; you love to think up new ways of doing things. Like a three, you are a social creature and love being around people and animals. Stability and security are important in your life and you always aim to make everything harmonious around you.

Like a star, you'll shine when you walk into a room, as others will find your communication skills captivating and interesting.

On a negative note, you could be a tad materialistic, paying more attention to possessions than you really should. Make an effort more often to share with others around you what you have.

5: The Magnet

If your name number makes you a five, you are one confident and self-assured person. You have a heightened sense of intuition, coupled with a talent for healing others with your touch or voice. You revel in daydreaming, allowing your thoughts to take you to distant places, but putting your thoughts into action is second nature too. You have the ability to start off with a dream, meet the challenges necessary to turn that dream into reality, and become a great success in life.

Consistency and stability are all-important to you, but even so, your love of adventure and travel play a huge role in your life, so expect to be jetting off to interesting locales.

There is something secretly special about you that others are drawn to. Your magnetic personality is an asset that will serve you well in life, but because you can be restless at times and become easily bored, you need to be mentally challenged, learning new skills to keep you grounded and in tune with earthly matters.

6: The Realist

Oh, boy, are sixes strong-minded and assertive! You certainly stick to your guns when you know you are right, and you rarely back down. You are there for anyone who needs you and are generous with your time and money, but to cross you is a big mistake. If pushed too far, you tend to be unforgiving and you stand your ground. You're patient up to a point, but no fool either.

Balance and order are enormously important to you, so your home is tidy and clean. Quiet times are essential for your peace of mind, and you love to bury your nose in a good book and lock yourself away for an hour or two.

Failure is not a word in your vocabulary. If you are faced with a challenge, you tackle it with vigor. You take a realistic view when beginning new projects, and you have the energy needed to get them done, but you should try not to be too opinionated and should try to understand that everyone has to go through life at their own pace.

7: The Visionary

Here we have an individual who is blessed with extraordinary abilities to see the future. You have excellent communication skills and you delight in a career that involves interacting with others.

You have a tremendous potential to right life's wrongs, and you may get angry or irritated when things are out of your control. Being an idealist, you have to be careful not to shoulder everyone's burdens; otherwise, you'll burn yourself out. You are sensitive, caring, and steady on your feet, but you can be thrown off balance by negative vibrations. Ambitious to the hilt, you're not afraid to branch out and reach your goals.

The downside of a seven personality? You may be a bit of a loner and perhaps even perceived as being aloof. If this bothers you (some people like to cultivate an air of mystery, others don't), just flash your grin. Smiles always warm up other people.

8: The Prophet

You are a complicated and interesting creature. To begin with, you are born with a sixth sense, but you need to develop your psychic focus to receive any messages that the universe sends to you. You have a tremendous ability to see beyond what is written and interpret what is not seen by the human eye. The prophet personality is strong-willed and determined and feels a need to change the world. Not only do you have a deep understanding of other people's needs, you're a delicate flower yourself, requiring nurturing and love.

Your mind is like an airplane propeller always in motion, churning around new ideas, and this makes you a person who sets trends and fashions. Your faults? You may push people aside if they stand in the way of your goals.

9: The Analyst

Analytical nines have no time to be bored. For you, there just aren't enough hours in the day to get everything done! You have a practical and methodical nature and are loyal and sincere. You're quick to learn and always put your thoughts into action to create an orderly and productive life.

Your heart is so big that you care deeply for strangers as well as friends and family. This makes you wise and accepting of all people, even (or especially) accepting of their faults. Keep your wise head firmly screwed on, though, because at times you can be a little too trusting of people. Usually, your unbelievable insight into the minds of others will kick in when you need it most, so you shouldn't go wrong too often. Being open-minded and interested in many subjects, you're likely to have a wide knowledge of all things.

When low or unhappy, nines tend to give in to vices and bad habits. Beware of this inclination and guard against it.

Number Name Games

One of the most frequent questions I am asked about numerology is "What happens if I don't like my name?" The beauty of numerology is that it works with you and your name changes and variants. It's not like an arranged marriage where you don't get to choose your mate. Choose the name you're most comfortable with and work with those digits. For example, let's say that the name on your birth certificate is Kathleen White, but you've always been called Kate, and though you gave up your maiden name years and years ago, you've always felt more connected to the surname White than to your married name. So to find your personality number, go with "Kate White." Likewise, if you've changed your name from Mary to Songbird (or Morningstar or Sunshine, for that matter), work with the name you feel most connected to. That's who you are in your heart; that's who you are in the universe. Note: If you do not use your middle name regularly, you can leave it out of the formula.

ADDING UP YOUR FATE: YOUR DESTINY AND YOU

Mastering your destiny number is another fascinating aspect of numerology. This number describes your strongest points and how to make your destiny work for you.

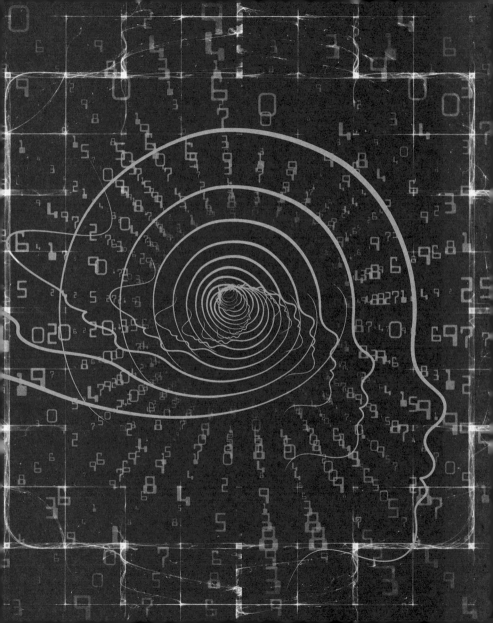

To find your destiny number, add the digits of the month, day, and year of your birth, using the same simple procedure you used to find your personality number. Let's say your birth date is 3/18/1984 and you want to find out what your physical and spiritual missions are on this life plane. Just add 3 + 1 + 8 + 1 + 9 + 8 + 4. This adds up to 34. Add those digits together to find your destiny number, like this: 3 + 4 = 7.

Now let's look at the breakdown below to see what destiny has in store for you:

Destiny Number 1

You have phenomenal leadership skills that will come in handy when you're climbing the corporate ladder to success. Never let anyone sway your convictions or talk you out of believing in your dreams. Follow your intuition and the rewards will be great.

Destiny Number 2

You have boundless energy and are filled with optimism and enthusiasm. These skills will serve you well in life. Your mission is to guide people by your own example and help them find a new road if they become lost in their own dream world and doubt their role in life. It's important to remember that, be it through art, music, writing, or teaching, you have much to give others in life.

Destiny Number 3

You have an innate sense of other people's problems, and your mission is to help those who have doubts about their capabilities find their true inner light. This road can be demanding. It will require you to have empathy,

understanding, and patience; however, since you are a natural caretaker, this
task is a perfect fit for you.

Destiny Number 4

You are a very positive person who connects to other happy-go-lucky souls.
However, be on the lookout for those who have faced personal tragedies and
need your helping hand. Your purpose is to become a passionate believer in your
inner power. You have the ability—by extending a helping hand with a calm and
healing voice—to help people recycle negative thinking into productive thoughts
that can heal their mind and spirit. Take advantage of every opportunity that
comes your way. Don't be afraid to step outside your comfort zone and reach for
the stars. By getting on the megaphone and not being afraid to speak your mind,
you will be able to make a difference in another person's life. This could mean
getting involved in politics or community affairs. There is a world out there
waiting to be explored, and you are limited only by your imagination.

Destiny Number 5

You are blessed with strong willpower and the determination to succeed.
These qualities will serve you well when you undertake new ventures or
get involved in projects that can improve the quality of other people's lives.
There will be times when you doubt yourself and feel the burdens of the
world weighing heavily upon your shoulders, but keep trudging onward.
The world is counting on you to realize your dreams!

Destiny Number 6

You are a great communicator—straightforward and honest. The world
needs someone like you to tell it the truth. You are also an innovator and

a motivator. With skills like these, you can succeed in politics or become a leader in community organizations that help people in need. You can also help save the planet by getting involved in "green" projects!

Destiny Number 7

You have the power and motivational qualities that inspire confidence in others. This suggests that you will go far in life, perhaps becoming a world leader or some other public figure. Certainly, the world is your oyster and you are the shining pearl that can light up the darkness in another person's life. Your true mission is to inspire, empower, and teach others to see beyond a stark black-and-white world.

Destiny Number 8

You have the visionary skills to see far into the future. You gravitate toward science, medicine, or writing, and you may make new discoveries or publish prophetic books. You will journey far and wide in your lifetime, unraveling the mysteries of life. You are also blessed with creative and communication skills, and you will use them to share your experiences with others, challenging them to reach for the stars!

Destiny Number 9

It is likely you will excel at anything in life that you want to do. You are detail-oriented, with leadership qualities that may allow you to walk among the giants in the corporate world. You're known as a mediator whose wisdom brings people of opposing views together. Your mission in life is twofold: to reach out to others and give them the confidence to succeed, and to encourage others to find the greater goodness within themselves.

BIRTHDAY SPELL MAGICK

You know you love your birthday. Even though your age creeps up, having your own special day never gets old.

Birthdays are also symbolically important. It is thought that the ritual of lighting candles started with a Greek tradition in honor of Artemis, goddess of the moon. Candles were placed on an altar, and if a person blew out all their birthday candles in one breath, then Artemis would grant their birthday wish.

Today, we still use this ancient tradition, although the altar has been replaced by a cake. While modern witches do participate in the birthday-cake-and-candle ceremony, we like to take it a step further. For us, a birthday marks a very special event: it is the one time during the year when the universal energies are perfectly balanced for us and we can invite powerful magick into our lives with little effort.

How does this magick spell work? It's simple! Take the year you were born and add its digits together, reducing it to a single digit. Then do the same for the present year. Add these two numbers together and you'll come up with your life number for the present year. The nice thing about life numbers is that they cycle through the years from 1 to 9—every year brings its own little surprises.

If you were born in 1980, add

$1 + 9 + 8 + 0 = 18$.

Then add $1 + 8 = 9$.

If the year is 2011, add $2 + 0 + 1 + 1 = 4$.

Add the two numbers together: $9 + 4 = 13$. Reduce to a single digit: $1 + 3 = 4$. Your life number in this example is four.

Once you have ascertained your life number, you can wait for your birthday to arrive, then cast a spell to enhance your life. As with most things magickal, life numbers correspond to different colors, so choose a candle in the appropriate color listed below for your future reference. In this example, your life number this year is one. This number corresponds to the color red and correlates to the Year of Discovery. To energize your candle, all you have to do is light it three feet away from something electrical, like your computer; you do not want to get too close as you want to avoid melting your laptop. Place a cup of water next to it. The candle will absorb the electrical energy coming from the appliance, adding to its magick and intensifying your life number for the year.

Let the candle burn for one hour, then concentrate on your wish for a few minutes and blow the candle out. By this point, the water will be electrically charged, so when you have made your wish, wash your hands in the magickal water to seal the spell.

CANDLES, COLORS, AND THE YEAR AHEAD

As promised, here is a little peek at what you can expect in connection with your life number. What does this year hold in store for you?

1: THE YEAR OF DISCOVERY
Candle Color: Red

This is a terrific year to explore new ideas and alternative ways of thinking. Relationships need some extra-special care, especially if you are critical or nitpicky with those you love. Adventure and rewards are in the cards, and you will receive lots of attention (and will more than likely enjoy great success) when starting new projects. Your creativity will know no bounds when you are reaching for a higher purpose in life, but be careful not to extend yourself so far that you become exhausted in trying to reach your dreams. The Year of

Discovery brings many highlights, but you must dig deep to find the inner truth within yourself.

2: THE YEAR OF ENLIGHTENMENT
Candle Color: Yellow

Full steam ahead—don't look back and dwell on past failures; instead, look ahead to a year filled with endless possibilities. Lucky you! You'll certainly be busier than you have been in some time. This is an incredible year to fire up your inner spirit and put your thoughts into action.

If you're looking for relationships, look no farther than the end of your nose. Mr. or Ms. Perfect-for-You could well be knocking at your door, so spruce yourself up and get a makeover. Career possibilities are also endless. Expect changes in the home or office, but don't push yourself too hard or you could run out of steam. You'll need to conserve your strength and energies to take on new projects, as many opportunities are just around the corner.

3: THE YEAR OF THE REALIST
Candle Color: White

You are an unstoppable force this year! Valuable lessons can and will be learned, which in turn will prompt you to seek out new avenues of exploration. Although your feet are planted firmly on the ground, make sure your head doesn't get lost in the clouds. This is a very important year to stay grounded and focused.

Your best efforts will shine when you take on new projects, but don't be surprised if you feel your life is like a roller coaster. Part and parcel of being a realist is experiencing the ups and downs in life and learning from past mistakes.

4: THE YEAR OF THE WISE ONE
Candle Color: Blue

This year, burned bridges will be mended and new bridges will be built for you to explore. It is also a year when new doors of opportunity open up to you. Your life will take on exciting new dimensions as you grow, mature, and change. Marvelous adventures will take you to new lands filled with mystery.

This is the year to make changes and not be afraid to take risks. You may be a dreamer, but never underestimate the power of your dreams to come true! This year you could be faced with other people's problems; be prepared to lend a hand to those asking for help. Your guidance will assist others and you'll be offering advice to those in need.

5: THE YEAR OF THE TRUTH SEEKER
Candle Color: White

This year everything finally seems clearer than it has in a long while! This is the time when you must consider what is right for you, so make a conscious effort to analyze your situation, starting with a spring cleaning for your life. (Out with the old—or with anything that just isn't serving you anymore.) The lesson here is to trust your inner feelings and separate yourself from people or situations that hinder your spirit.

If you play your cards right, career opportunities will abound! This is a potentially busy year with many unexpected events. Stay on your toes, but make sure you don't step on anyone else's little piggies in the pursuit of your goals. Love comes from strange and unusual places, and you could find your sweetheart literally standing next to you in the supermarket checkout line.

6: THE YEAR OF THE SEEKER
Candle Color: Pink

This year, you need to exercise a certain amount of restraint when faced with opposing views. You could do well in your career if you believe in yourself. You can rely on the strength of loved ones and friends, whose advice will see you through some tough situations.

Romance is in the air, and you just might meet your significant other if you're realistic in your expectations (so stop waiting for the latest heartthrob to call and give that guy in accounting a shot). Be prepared for unexpected changes in the home. If you are thinking of moving, this is a good year to start looking for that perfect property. Take care with your health and make sure that you are eating right, getting enough sleep, and not abusing your body. Self-indulgence will only deplete your energy this year and make you feel powerless.

7: THE YEAR OF THE DREAMER
Candle Color: Purple

One of the most significant features of the Year of the Dreamer is prophetic dreaming—dreams that come true! You may start to take more of an interest in spiritual matters, so create a dream diary or learn the tarot.

New friends will be circulating in your orbit, and romance will tick along nicely. This is also the year when you can make radical changes in your lifestyle, such as going back to school, finding a new job, or going for a promotion. Your memory and concentration may not be at their best, so you could overlook or underestimate a potentially important event. Set realistic targets and focus on hitting them!

8: THE YEAR OF EMPOWERMENT
Candle Color: Gold

This is the year when you will learn from your biggest mistakes. (Now, now, don't grumble—learning is *always* an opportunity!) It is also a time when your resume needs some fine-tuning because of unexpected problems in the workplace.

Be assured that despite these challenges, things can and will work out for you as long as you continue to believe in yourself.

Family matters will also be in the spotlight, and you will be called upon to help someone in need. Animals will play an important role in the coming year, and you may take on a new pet or help an animal in distress. The Year of Empowerment is also significant when it comes to turning corners and meeting up with new responsibilities, all of which you can handle because you are resilient and have a reservoir of inner strength.

Your love life will be up and down, but be patient. You may not be content in love at the moment but . . . good things come to those who wait!

9: THE YEAR OF CONTENTMENT
Candle Color: Green

The 9 year is the completion of the numerological cycle, and it brings with it happiness and joy. (The best birthday gifts of all!) It's a time to plant the seeds for your future, keeping in mind that as you sow, so shall you reap. It is important that you keep your thoughts pure and positive, because your final destination is cosmic bliss.

One of your lessons this year is to break the monotony of having a closed mind and to become open to embracing new ideas. Career, home, love, and relationships take on a whole new meaning during this time in the life cycle; decisions made during this period will follow you as you go around the numerological wheel time and time again! Luck is on your side and everything you touch turns to gold. Share not only your time, but also your good fortune, and your karmic wheel will continue to turn in a positive way.

Leanna's Tip

There are many different ways to work with numbers and numerology. So, if you have a desire to study the subject further, either Google it or pop into a metaphysical shop and take a look at their reading material. Most of all, learn to see numbers as representations of a larger truth—the truth of who you are and what's to come. All of that adds up to a promising future, my friend!

CHAPTER 15

SHAWN

DREAM A LITTLE DREAM

THERE I WAS, WALKING DOWN A STREET paved with ice cream, wearing my tiara and a pair of diamond-soled shoes. Carrying a bag full of money, I was strewing bills like rose petals. I stopped to pick up my pet tiger at the kennel before going home to my fairy-tale castle in the clouds. Just then I was awakened with a start and muttered, "Oh, darn that alarm clock!"

Dreams can be most simply described as sequences of images and sensations that we experience most often when we are in deep REM (rapid eye movement) sleep. Everyone dreams, even though you probably know people who say, "I do *not* dream! I go to sleep and I wake up eight hours later without ever having one." The difference is that some of us remember our dreams and some of us recall absolutely nothing.

Most of us love a good night's sleep filled with all sorts of adventures and escapades. You probably know that you can use your dreams as a kind of mirror to understand what's bothering you in the daylight hours—but did you know that you can actually manipulate your dreams in order to visit different dimensions? The different dimensions one can visit are called "time warping." You can visit the past, present, or future. Sometimes you may even see "ghost lights" as I have seen numerous times when staying in haunted houses. For centuries, Wiccans have known the secret to making dreams come true—and it starts with controlling the dream itself.

DREAM TEAMS

In ancient Egypt, people believed that dreams were messages sent from the gods. These could be warnings of impending doom or harbingers of good things to come. The Egyptians were so fascinated by these nighttime dispatches that they created "dream books." Written on papyrus, the books were encyclopedias of dream symbols and interpretations. The ancient Egyptians also participated in the intriguing practice of "dream incubation":

A person who needed guidance from a particular deity would visit the god's temple or shrine to take part in prayer and ritual, then sleep in the temple in order to receive a divine dream. In the morning, the petitioner would consult a priest about the images that had been incubated during the night, and the two of them would spend hours unraveling the messages in those symbols.

The writers of the Bible, too, recorded stories of people receiving revelations from God in their dreams, such as the passage in Genesis about Jacob, the grandson of Abraham and brother of Esau. While he was sleeping one night, Jacob dreamed of a ladder that reached all the way to heaven, from which God spoke to him.

In the sixteenth century, religious clerics theorized that if the devil appeared to you in dreams or if you had any impure dreams, then you must have the devil within you. Understandably, this idea sent lots of people into a panic; surely, if they had the devil within them, their nighttime visions were going to send them straight to hell!

Finally, in the nineteenth century, a French doctor named Alfred Maury formed many theories that laid the groundwork for modern-day dream interpretation. He hypothesized that external stimuli are the catalysts for dreams, including issues that confront us during our waking hours.

DREAMING THE FUTURE

According to sleep scientists, dreams are just a way for the subconscious to sort out some of the more confusing things that happen over the course of a typical day. This doesn't really seem logical when you're dreaming of climbing banana trees with a gang of monkey friends (unless, of course, this is what you do for fun during your waking hours), but that's where dream interpretation symbols can help. I'll give you the lowdown on these a little later in this chapter.

However, some dreams feel less like odd nighttime adventures and more like real life. And when you dream of something disturbing that's related to your daily life, it's worth taking a good, hard look at that dream. You could be getting a sneak peek at what's to come.

SUBCONSCIOUS REALITY

Who doesn't love a good dream? Whether you're sitting on a beach with a handsome man or a beautiful woman, strutting your stuff on a runway in

Paris, or flying without the help of a jetpack, a great dream can feel like a real adventure, inspiring you and lifting your spirits all day long.

Bad dreams, on the other hand, can be totally disruptive. First, they can prevent you from getting a good night's sleep, which makes you cranky and less productive the following day. Second, the emotions associated with negative dreams can be very real. If you dream that your better half has dumped you or is having a wild affair, you might walk around the next day feeling genuinely despondent. This reaction is due in part to the fact that you are actually experiencing the emotions of the dream or empathizing with it in some way. Even though the events didn't happen during your waking hours, emotionally you have reacted in the same way you would have if those events really did happen. Most of the time these dreams stem from some deep-seated fear within you, but it could also be that you are having a premonition or a precognition that something upsetting is going to happen.

So let's look at the example of being dumped by your boyfriend in your dream. Even though it hasn't really happened, it's worth exploring your subconscious to figure out why you had that dream in the first place. Is it possible that you:

* Are insecure in your relationship and fear he may be bored with you?
* Think he's stepping out on you with someone else?
* Believe he's getting ready to break up with you?
* Are actually ready to move on without him but haven't admitted it to yourself yet?

In cases like these, your dream may have handed you a vision of what's around the corner. Should you choose to accept this, then perhaps now is a good time to get to the bottom of it, probably by having a long conversation with your guy about what's really going on with the two of you.

This is not to say that all precognitions are bad. You might dream of a job promotion, winning a marathon, or becoming a famous actress, and find that in a short space of time you're on your way to success.

IN YOUR WILDEST DREAMS

Precognitions are neat little packages of the future that the universe delivers when we least expect it. However, there is a way we can control our dreams— and maybe even organize our future by creating positive visions.

Lucid dreaming is a way to remain consciously in control of your dreams. You tell your mind what's going to happen next; if the dream veers off into unacceptable territory, then you steer it back to where you want it. Usually, the dream starts off on its own—because you have to allow the subconscious mind some control. Once you become alert to the fact that it is a dream, you can then do whatever you feel like within it.

Some people use lucid dreams to prevent recurring nightmares; others use it to address self-esteem issues or to practice ways to handle a certain situation, anything from telling off a nosy neighbor to negotiating the purchase of a car. You can use this technique to dream up new spells and infuse them with your own spirit. Here's a step-by-step guide:

1. Start by becoming more aware of your state of mind in the days before attempting a lucid dream. Stop yourself every now and then and say,

"I'm awake. This is what's happening." You're just training your mind to recognize what is taking place at that moment.

2. Before you go to bed, follow a soothing, relaxing bedtime routine. Take a hot shower, put on comfortable nightclothes, and find your favorite blanket—whatever is going to allow you to drift off comfortably.

3. When you lie down, concentrate on feeling yourself supported by the bed. You want to relax every single part of your body. Breathe slowly and deeply.

4. Now repeat to yourself, "I can control my dreams. I can control my dreams." If you want to dream of something specific, try "I'm going to dream about _____."

Hopefully all this relaxation will allow you to slip right into your dream. When you begin the dreaming process, simply say to yourself, "I'm in charge here, and *this* is what's going to happen." Obviously, nothing is off limits, so make the most of it! Try out things you would never—or could never—do in your daytime life!

SLEEP YOUR WAY TO SUCCESS

I mentioned above that some people use lucid dreams to improve their self-esteem. Coaches and therapists have long advised their players and clients to use visualization to encourage successful outcomes. Visualization is really just a form of meditation, but since meditation is often described as a dreamlike state, it's fair game for our discussion here.

Let's say there's a house that you are desperate to buy. You're in a bidding war with two other potential buyers, and you just have to find a way to make it your own. Here's what to do to help ensure that you end up signing that deed:

1. Prepare for meditation. Sit or lie in a quiet room, free of distractions. Light candles or incense, play some soothing music, and close your eyes.
2. Breathe deeply—in through the nose, out through the mouth.
3. Feel every part of your body relax and just give in to it.
4. When you're as limp as a noodle, start your visualization. View the house as though you're standing at the end of the driveway. Walk up the drive and unlock the front door with the key. Enter the house. Walk through each room, seeing your furniture and belongings as they will be when you live there. Sit on the couch. Kick your shoes off. Be in the moment in your new home.

When you open your eyes, congratulate yourself for closing the deal on the perfect place to live—be in the moment. That's yours to keep, but you have to make sure to store it correctly. Don't let doubt enter your mind; just know that things are going to work out in your favor; then behave that way in your dealings. We attract the same kind of energy we put out to the world; visualization just helps you to solidify that energy so it will be there when you need it.

DREAM JOURNALS

A really great way to enhance positive feelings from lucid dreaming and visualization is to keep a dream journal. Journals are also useful for keeping track of recurring dreams, especially those that are full of vague symbols you just can't make heads or tails of. Journals can help you organize patterns of information and lead you to moments of discovery when you're able to say, "Oh, so *that's* why I'm dreaming about talking penguins!"

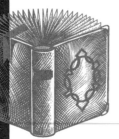

A dream journal can be any kind of notebook—the one caveat is that it has to fit on your nightstand. And you absolutely must keep a writing implement with it. You and I both know you aren't going to get up to search for a pencil when you wake up from a dream at three in the morning, and believe me, you will *not* remember the details of that dream when your alarm goes off at seven.

WHAT KIND OF INFORMATION GOES IN THE JOURNAL?

The date, the time you went to bed, and anything significant—good, bad, or unusual—that happened during the day: these are the kinds of things you should note down before you hit the hay. Also, if you ate late at night or had something to eat that didn't sit well with you, include that too. Stomach upsets can wreak havoc on sleep and dream states, as can certain medications, so make a note of everything.

As soon as you wake up—whether it's in the middle of the night or in the morning—try to stay still. The less external stimulation you have, the better. Close your eyes and try to remember where your mind just came back from. If you're afraid you're going to fall back asleep and be late for work, before you go to bed be sure to set your alarm to go off a little earlier so you'll be able to hit the snooze button and take the time to retrace your dream steps. If you can grab on to any little detail of your dream, then go with it. Often one piece of information will lead you right back into your nighttime adventures. Stay in your unfocused state and go as far into recall as you can.

When you can't go any further, open your eyes, grab your journal, and write. Don't worry about making a coherent story out of it, and don't worry about punctuation and spelling—just spit it all out. There will be time for analysis later.

You can also use a voice recorder to capture your initial impressions, but I think it's really important to have a written record of your dreams. It just makes it easier to recognize repetitive information and discern meaningful patterns.

DREAM SYMBOLS

Everybody dreams, even those who insist they don't, but everybody dreams differently. The reason is obvious: dreams are a reflection of the influences on the subconscious mind, and everybody has their own unique issues that manifest as nighttime nuttiness. But even though we all produce our own visions, there are some common recurring dream themes, like flying or standing naked in a crowd. What do these mean?

FLYING: Flying is a reflection of your capabilities and suggests a sense of freedom. This means you *know* you can do it (whatever "it" is).
FALLING: Falling with fear means you're feeling out of control or insecure. Enjoying the fall means that you're ready to take on new challenges.
TEST-TAKING: Taking a test means you're struggling with learning something or feeling insecure in your knowledge of something.

NAKEDNESS: Naked in public in your dream? You're feeling vulnerable.

TEETH: If your teeth are falling out in your dreams, it means you're feeling insecure romantically, you're worried about health issues, or you've been saying things you shouldn't during your waking hours. It can also be an omen of grave illness or even a death for someone you know.

STORMY WEATHER: Storm dreams indicate that you're feeling overwhelmed or angry.

CEMETERIES: To dream of walking through a cemetery means that you are sad or fearful. But don't despair—it can also mean that you're on the verge of a rebirth of some sort!

Now, when we get into talking about less common symbols, I could go on forever. There are entire books written about dream symbolism, so I'm only going to discuss symbols that I feel are significant. If you don't find what you're looking for here, you can either do a simple Internet search ("dream symbols") or head to the library or bookstore to find a more complete listing.

See if any of these symbols speak to you in the dark of the night:

RESTROOMS: Dreaming of bathrooms means that you need more privacy in your daytime life (or it may mean you need to use the bathroom and your body is giving you a hint to wake you up).

GARDEN: A garden of flowers indicates love and happiness in your life. A garden filled with weeds means that you need to clear your head regarding a spiritual issue.

CELEBRATIONS AND PARTIES: If you dream of a party, you're achieving your goals.

ABANDONMENT: Dreams where you're left behind mean that you need to let go of old beliefs and habits.

KIDNAPPING: If you're being abducted in your dream, someone is exerting control over you—and you don't like it!

ACCIDENT: Dreaming of an accident is a reflection of an anxious state of mind. What are you worried about or scared of?

ADULTERY: If you dream you're cheating on your significant other, it could simply mean that you're mixed up in something unpleasant—but not necessarily an affair.

DEATH: If you dream of your own death, you're going through a life transition.

RUNNING: If you're running from someone in your dream, you're really avoiding something in your life that you're afraid to face. If you are running toward something it means you are trying to reach a goal in your life.

RINGS: A ring in your dream is a good sign—it symbolizes loyalty and wholeness in your life. If the ring is broken, that's not so good. It means that someone is questioning your dedication.

BASEMENTS: Going into a cellar in your dream indicates that you're suppressing some emotion or fear.

CELEBRITIES: If Lady Gaga or one of her celebrity friends show up in your dreams, it means that you will come into good luck soon.

BEING CHASED: A dream where someone is hot on your tail means that you're unwilling to see another point of view on an important topic.

PREGNANCY: Being with child in your dream suggests not that you are actually pregnant, but that you're growing in some aspect of your life.

WATER: Water that is clear and smooth on the surface in your dream indicates peace of mind. Murky water suggests that negative emotions are nagging you.

FINDING SOMETHING: When you find something in your dream, it means that you're acknowledging part of yourself that you've been ignoring—maybe a newfound aspect of spirituality or a shift in your beliefs.

WAR: Dreaming of war suggests that your waking hours are full of distress and chaos.

This is just a partial list of dream symbols to get you started on dream interpretation. There are many dream symbol books on the market to help you learn more. I would suggest reserving a section of your dream journal for notes on symbols and what they mean. After you have a strange dream, look up the images and their meanings and write them down so that the next time they appear in your dreams, you won't have to hunt through pages of journal entries to find their meaning.

ASTRAL PROJECTION

One of the dream symbols I just mentioned was death, but you'll notice I only talked about dreaming of your own death. When you dream of someone who has already died, there may be more to the picture than meets the "subconscious" eye. In fact, these may not be dreams at all. A person from the other side may have used astral projection to contact you.

Some people can develop a skill called astral projection, which is something like dreaming, in that the subconscious mind takes over—but in astral projection, your spirit actually leaves this earthly plane and enters into a different reality. Basically, astral projection is a way of releasing your spirit from your body and letting it fly free. Just watch out for birds and low-flying planes!

Astral projection can be used to visit loved ones on the other side, to relive moments you wish you could get back, or to gain knowledge from spirit guides. It may sound very supernatural and mysterious to you, but bear with me. This is another type of creative visualization, so even if you aren't completely sure that you want to leave this world and enter other dimensions, think of it as a way to open your mind and explore its limits.

To give astral projection a whirl, begin by following the same steps you would for meditation. Find a quiet spot, light candles, play music, burn incense, and breathe deeply. Then follow the steps below:

1. Imagine a beam of white light shooting from your feet right up through the top of your head. White light is always used for protection from sinister spirits or entities, and it will be important for this little journey you're about to take.

2. Say a prayer for protection.

3. Imagine yourself tethered to your bed or to the ground with a cord made of "white" or "pure" energy. Wiccans and psychics use what some might call white or pure energy to keep their souls attached to their bodies while in the dream state.

4. Feel your spirit (or your soul or "second body," as some people call it)

lift and rise out of your physical body. Nothing can impede it—you can rise right through the ceiling, through the apartment above you, through the roof, and then go anywhere you want.

5. If you encounter your spirit guides when you're out of your body, go ahead and talk to them. Ask them anything you want—that's why you're in this state.

6. If you feel scared, just remember that cord that's keeping you bound to the physical plane. You can always simply say, "I want to go back now" and return to your body.

Some people experience a jolt or a sense of falling when they are just about to project. This may be because, as one theory puts it, the spirit doesn't gently float upward when it is leaving your body, but actually moves down into your back, out to the side, and then up. Have you ever been drifting off to sleep and then awakened with a start? This is when you know that you are on the brink of leaving your body.

Leanna has been experimenting with this for many years and is very skilled at astral projection, so she can go off at a moment's notice. She sees multicolored lights dancing behind her closed eyelids just before she goes on one of her travels. Once you get the hang of entering into this state, explore it. Talk to your spirit guides about the issues that concern you—your job, your family, how you're going to pay the rent next month, where you should go on vacation. There's nothing you can't do, nowhere you can't go, and nothing you can't ask! And since some spirit guides are thousands of years old, you may return home with information and advice you would never hear from anyone else.

To make your dreams less chaotic and help your astral journey go smoothly, light a white candle an hour before bedtime and drink a cup of herbal tea (chamomile is a good one to try as it is known for its relaxing properties). When you have finished the tea, blow out the candle. This will heighten your vibration and cleanse your energies before you head off to the astral plane.

MAKE THE MOST OF DREAM TIME

Now that you have learned some neat little Wiccan dreaming tricks, I hope you'll never look at sleep the same way again. When you lie down at night, you aren't necessarily turning everything off until the sun comes back up—you can be sorting out your feelings, resolving confusion, and experiencing amazing adventures while your physical body takes some time out. So let your mind go and let your sleepy spirit fly free—you never know where you'll end up.

CHAPTER 16

SHAWN

DIVINE
DIVINING

QUESTIONS, QUESTIONS, QUESTIONS . . . all of us are plagued by the unknown from time to time. Should you take this new job or hold out for a better offer? Is this new love interest worth your while, or are you kidding yourself? Is Monday the best day to fly standby, or should you wait till Tuesday . . . or Thursday? The way I look at it, I'm just happy to get through airport security wearing my sterling silver pentagram without setting off the metal detector!

At times, we all have a sense that something we are planning or thinking about isn't quite right. Maybe you aren't sure why you don't want to travel on a certain day, for example, but you just know the idea isn't sitting well with you. It could be that you are remembering the strange guy you had to sit next to on your last flight, or it could be just your imagination going wild. But often our intuition reports back to us with a little tug on the sleeve, as if to say, "Hey! Pay attention! I need to tell you something!"

THE PENDULUM, PAST AND PRESENT

For those of us who are in tune with our intuitive side, the simple little tool that is the pendulum can help us dig deeper into our inner self and be guided by our inner voice in finding the best paths to follow. Using the pendulum is actually a form of *dowsing*, which is also sometimes called divining. If you're familiar with these terms, you might envision someone running around Death Valley with a forked stick, looking for water. That is one form of dowsing, the one that for some reason sticks in the public's mind. In fact, dowsing with a pendulum is a much more common practice than using a stick or divining rod, and there are many other methods as well. While you can certainly use a pendulum to seek water, it is more commonly used to divine truth, to balance energy, to cleanse the chakras, or to make contact with the spiritual plane for any number of reasons.

Dowsing itself is simply a means of using your body's own intuition and reflexes to understand what's happening in your life and in your environment. In interpreting your readings, you're really just learning to look at things in a new way—a way that's always been accessible to you, though perhaps you weren't actively using it before.

Dowsing has been around forever. There are indications that it was used many centuries ago to appease the gods, to predict the future, to find auspicious times for sowing and reaping, and to be judge and jury in matters of the law (specifically, in determining a suspect's guilt or innocence).

In 1326, Pope John XXII authorized the prosecution of sorcerers as devil-worshipping heretics and forbade divining as an act of sorcery. There are no statistics on how many Catholics continued to perform dowsing rituals in secret, but since the practice has survived to this day, I imagine it was more than a few. I'm also not sure why the Pope thought Satan would waste his time answering questions about such matters as the best time to plant a harvest.

An old wives' tale says that the pendulum can predict the sex of an unborn baby. A dowser or psychic would tie the pregnant woman's wedding ring to a length of string and dangle it over her big belly. The ring's movement was supposed to indicate a boy or a girl (if a pendulum swung to the left, it was a boy; to the right, a girl). In Britain the same method is still used today, but the ring is replaced with a threaded needle. I'll talk more about how to interpret the swing of the pendulum later in this chapter.

IN PURSUIT OF THE PERFECT PENDULUM

A pendulum is an object that hangs on a string or chain. The object can be made of wood, metal, plastic, or even a string. It can be adorned with crystals or unadorned. The weight of the object is not important. Most dowsers will tell you that it's important to find a pendulum you will be comfortable with.

Pendulums are not hard to come by. Most metaphysical stores stock them, and you can also purchase them easily online. They are available in every price range, from under $10 to over $100. Think of it as choosing a wise new friend, one you'll be seeking guidance and advice from. This is not a decision to make quickly or lightly. It's just like selecting a crystal for yourself; you have to feel a genuine connection to get the best results.

PENDULUM PROPERTIES

So you waltz into your local metaphysical shop, ready to adopt the perfect pendulum, and you look into the jewelry case only to find there are over fifty to choose from. All colors, all sizes—how do you begin the process of elimination?

First, ask the shopkeeper for help. Most men and women who work in these stores are extremely knowledgeable about the products and how to use them, and most are also eager to share their own experiences. Listen to what they have to say, but keep in mind that the pendulum is a very personal experience, so what works well for one person may not work for you.

Pendulums come in all weights, shapes, and designs. Generally speaking, beginners should start with a medium weight. The theory is that a pendulum that's too light can pick up too many energies and send mixed messages. A too-heavy weight can be difficult to learn with because it takes longer for the pendulum to gain momentum, which means that its reaction time is slower. This could leave you feeling frustrated.

The shape you choose will depend on what you want to use it for:

SPIRAL: A pointy-ended, spiral-shaped weight, used for answering general life questions.

TRIANGULAR: This kind of pendulum picks up the vibration of numbers, and is great for use in numerology or choosing lottery numbers.

SEPHOROTON: A pendulum that has a circular center and a pointed bottom. This unique shape is supposed to cut down on errant vibrations and give clear answers to questions about health, love, and money.

MERKABA: A star-shaped pendulum that incorporates sacred geometry in its design to unite the body, soul, and spirit. This union creates an energetic field called the Merkaba effect.

CHAKRA: A stone pendulum whose chain contains seven stones representing the seven chakras (the body's energy centers). Used to find and repair an imbalance in one or more of the chakras.

OSIRIS: A long pendulum with four "hemispheres" stacked on top of each other. This design is meant to amplify the pendulum's sensitivity, and the osiris is considered to be a very powerful tool. It is used to research electromagnetic fields, detect viruses in the body, and gain insight into astrological charts.

CHAMBERED: A hollow pendulum that you can place energetic crystals inside for greater power and clarity. If you're asking the pendulum a question about another person, you can also place a strand of that person's hair in the chamber.

Now let's talk about the materials that pendulums are made of, the energy qualities of different stones and crystals, and why you might choose one over another (for more information about crystals and stones, see chapter 8, "Crystal Power"):

QUARTZ is a universal stone, which means that it responds well to whatever purpose you assign it. It draws, activates, stores, transmits, and multiplies all kinds of energetic forces, so no matter what you're using a quartz pendulum for—questions of love, money, social responsibility, research—you can't go wrong.
ROSE QUARTZ is sometimes recommended for women, as it has a special vibration that

reacts well to feminine energy. Rose quartz emits love, compassion, and forgiveness, promotes creativity and confidence, and heals emotional and sexual issues.

AMETHYST is used in meditation, channeling, and focusing psychic abilities. It gives a feeling of peace and connects you with your spiritual side.

CITRINE clears negative energy in a big way! After using citrine, you may notice you feel more optimistic, energetic, focused, and confident. Citrine also attracts abundance (which can go a long way toward making you feel more optimistic and confident).

LAPIS LAZULI connects the physical and celestial planes, increasing wisdom and otherworldly knowledge, awareness, and intuition. Lapis lazuli is also a stone of protection.

FLUORITE promotes stability, order, balance, and healing, and it is a great stone for use in matters where clarity and objectivity are important. Fluorite doesn't absorb energy the way other stones do, so it gives pretty reliable responses.

MOONSTONE emits a feminine energy, supporting balance, intuition, and good judgment. Moonstone is also used to balance the female reproductive system and to protect travelers on their journeys.

BLOODSTONE is the stone of courage, promoting centering, grounding, and balance. This is a good stone to use for anxiety or emotional stress.

Remember that an inexpensive pendulum will work just as well as a pricier version. The crux of the matter really is in learning to focus and concentrate your energy. Although there are purists out there who believe that you should only use certain crystals or shapes for certain purposes, most people say that choosing and using a pendulum is a very personal thing. In other words, if you find that a pendulum is responding well for you, don't worry so much about its material, shape, or price. As with all things spiritual, it's best to just go with the flow.

GET TO KNOW YOUR PENDULUM

The pendulum responds to your energetic field, but because it's a piece of rock, crystal, metal, or wood hanging from a chain, it also responds to gravity and reflexes. Obviously, you don't want to set the stone swinging by a flick of the wrist or a flinch of the fingers, so learning to hold the pendulum is an important step.

The reason I want you to understand this concept is that I don't want you to get false readings and then decide that the pendulum is a bogus tool. I don't want you buying into skeptics' beliefs that there is nothing beyond this earthly realm, that believers in the mystical planes create their own answers. The etheric realm is real, and you can tap into it.

To hold the pendulum correctly, position the chain between your thumb and forefinger, allowing the weight to dangle. If your pendulum has a long chain, it's perfectly all right to shorten it by holding it closer to the pendulum. Shortening the length also shortens response time.

Even though you should be friendly and comfortable with your pendulum, a pendulum session calls for a certain amount of focus and respect as well. Begin every session by settling into a quiet, calm space. Clear your mind. Invite your spirit guides and angels to join and assist you. Envision yourself surrounded by a white light, and say a simple, silent prayer for protection.

Remember that the pendulum does not respond to your mental urgings; instead, it responds to your energy. Negative, skeptical energy will result in negative findings. Positive, relaxed energy is what you want to put out for the best results.

When you're relaxed and your mind is clear and focused, ask your pendulum questions that it can answer "yes" to, easy things such as "Is it raining today?" or "Is my shirt pink?" Take note of how the pendulum responds to these easy queries. That's your "yes" motion. Once it starts moving, ask the pendulum to show you an even stronger "yes," perhaps by asking it, "Is my name _____?" so that there's no mistaking its movement. But if you don't get a more pronounced motion, don't fret.

Now ask the pendulum some "no" questions, like "Is my hair red?" (if you happen to be blond) or "Is today Saturday?" when you know it is Monday. Then ask it a "maybe" question, such as "Will I talk to my friend Joe today?" Notice how your pendulum reacts to these questions too.

The movement of the pendulum is obviously limited by physical factors, but you may discern several types of motion. Here's what to look for when you're waiting for an answer:

* A side-to-side swinging
* A diagonal swinging
* A clockwise or counterclockwise rotation
* A "jump"

Will your "yes" movement be the same from now until the end of time? Does the pendulum ever change its mind? Movements do change from time to time, so every now and then, especially once you really know your pendulum, retest it with your easy questions, just to make sure you're getting the same results.

If you want more of a visual response, you can hold the pendulum over a mat or card with answers printed on it. You can buy these or make these—though if you do create one on your own, make sure you leave plenty of room between the answer areas so you aren't confused by the pendulum's movements. One simple version of this mat has YES printed on the top and bottom, NO on the sides, and MAYBE in two diagonal corners. This setup encourages the pendulum to move in certain directions according to its responses.

Leanna's Tip

When you work with the pendulum, it doesn't usually tap into the lower vibrations, so there is little danger of invoking any unwanted spirits. However, when you are working with any form of divination, I do think it is nice to begin your spiritual session with a silent prayer for protection. You can do this by simply closing your eyes and asking your angel to protect you from anything negative and to surround you with a positive light.

ASK ANYTHING (BUT ASK THE RIGHT WAY)

You can ask your pendulum almost anything, but the way you phrase the question is important when it comes to understanding the larger picture. You have to understand that the pendulum can only give you "yes" and "no" answers, so it's pointless asking it something lengthy or intricate. This will just confuse matters, and you may not get any results at all.

For example, if you ask, "Should I buy a house now?" and the answer is "no," don't give up. You might be able to find out more by rephrasing your question. Try "Should I buy a house in the winter?" and see what happens. If you need to, go through each season and see which one the pendulum responds positively to.

Sometimes the pendulum won't swing at all, but will just hang there, showing no movement. This usually occurs when it doesn't know the answer to your question or when, for whatever reason, you are not supposed to know the outcome of a situation. You just have to accept this and change your subject to ask it something else.

If you make your questions as clear and concise as possible, the pendulum can more or less get to the bottom of anything:

* Questions about significant others
* Where to go on vacation
* Which outfit to wear to a job interview
* How much money to invest
* The best time to have children
* What kind of pet you should adopt
* Which career path to follow

You can even ask the best day to play golf or the best movie to see. There is *no* question that's off limits!

SWING INTO BETTER HEALTH

The pendulum is also used to single out health and emotional issues, many of which are believed to be tied to the chakras, or the energy centers of the body.

Pendulum energy can pinpoint imbalances in the chakras so that they can be restored to good health.

Chakra is a Sanskrit word meaning "wheel" or "turning." Both yogic Hindu and Tantric Buddhist philosophies teach that every human has these wheels of energy at seven specific points in the body along a column that goes from the base of the spine to the top of the head.

FIRST CHAKRA
Base or Root Chakra

Located at the base of the spine; relates to feelings of survival and feeling grounded. Imbalance makes you feel as though you have to fight to survive or as though you have no real grounding place.

SECOND CHAKRA
Sacral Chakra

Located near the ovaries in women, near the prostate in men; associated with sexual health. Blockage results in emotional issues or sexual guilt.

THIRD CHAKRA
Solar Plexus Chakra

Around the navel and lower torso; relates to feeling powerful in your surroundings. An imbalance makes you feel victimized, angry, and powerless.

FOURTH CHAKRA
Heart Chakra

Located right where you'd expect it to be. Relates to feeling loved and at peace with oneself and the world. An imbalance can actually manifest as heart or immune problems or lead you to feel as though you lack compassion for others.

FIFTH CHAKRA
Throat Chakra

Throat and neck region; linked to feelings of creativity and communication. Imbalance happens when you can't make yourself heard, and it manifests as discomfort in this area.

SIXTH CHAKRA
Brow or Third Eye Chakra

In the center of the forehead (pineal gland or third eye); relates to psychic abilities, imagination, and dreaming. An imbalance could result in writer's block or a general lack of ideas or vision.

SEVENTH CHAKRA
Crown Chakra

Located on the top of the head, associated with spiritual connection, understanding, and bliss. Imbalance results in feelings of floundering or just not knowing what you believe.

The chakras are the points for the gathering and transmitting of energy in the body, and as long as they are clear and balanced, *you'll* feel clear and balanced. If a chakra becomes imbalanced or blocked with negative energy, then you're going to feel it, either physically (as with a blocked throat chakra) or emotionally (as with a blocked crown chakra). But all is not lost! The pendulum can help to clear those problem areas, leaving you as balanced as an Olympic gymnast.

So how do you determine which chakras are clear as a bell and which are stagnant? You'll need a partner for this exercise—one who is not self-conscious and who doesn't mind sprawling out in a prone position. First you will assess your friend's chakras. Have your friend lie down face up on the floor or a bed, and sit beside them. Both of you should close your eyes and breathe to focus your energy and clear your minds of distractions. When you're both ready, begin by holding your pendulum over your friend's root chakra. (It's actually located near their rear end, but you can access the energy by holding it over their genital region . . . which is why you shouldn't choose a shy friend for this experiment.) Ask, "Is this chakra in balance?" Repeat the question until the answer becomes clear. Take note of the response, then move up the body, asking the same question over the other six chakras. Use the chakra list above to interpret what's going on with your friend.

If you should find that a chakra is out of whack, take your pendulum and move it in a clockwise motion over the area. This "stirs" the chakra, allowing whatever is stuck to begin moving and, hopefully, to be cleared out.

Now ask your friend to perform the same sequence of steps to evaluate your chakras.

THE CARE AND "FEEDING" OF YOUR PENDULUM

It is important to keep your pendulum clean, especially if it is made of crystal. A monthly cleansing is usually all it needs, but if you are using it to balance chakras, then I advise you to go through the cleansing procedure outlined below after each session.

Now, I have to make this clear: You can't cleanse your pendulum by tossing it into the dishwasher or leaving it in the pocket of your dirty jeans when you're doing the laundry. Of course, use a soft cloth to wipe off any smudges or dust, but be aware that energetic forces are the toughest "stains" you'll ever have to remove from your pendulum, so it must be done right. You'll need to use the strongest elements at your disposal—the elements of nature:

EARTH: Simply bury your pendulum in soil, sand, or sea salt and just let it sit for a few hours. (You can even do this indoors using a bowl.) The negative energies will be released and absorbed into the earthen element. If you do bury the pendulum in a bowl, just make sure to get rid of the soil, sand, or salt when you're finished. Take it outside and pour it right onto the earth.

FIRE: Place your pendulum in direct sunlight early in the morning. Let it sit until sundown to allow the positive energy to take hold.

WATER: This method requires a glass of water that's been energized by a crystal. (To do this, I recommend placing a crystal of quartz in a container of water and letting it soak for about twelve hours.) Put your pendulum in the energized water and allow it to sit in there for several hours.

AIR: Light a sandalwood incense stick and pass the pendulum through its smoke three times. Since you are directly involved in this process, you need to really focus on the task at hand, saying a prayer for cleansing or blessing or just stating your intent. When the pendulum feels light and solid (as opposed to heavy or "fuzzy"), the cleansing is complete.

Your Future Is in Motion

When using your pendulum to make decisions, you're going to feel a sense of control over your world that's nothing less than amazing. Why should a stone or crystal make you feel as though you're finally seeing things for what they are and what they can be? Because the pendulum is just a means of putting you in touch with what you already know. So connect with that knowledge, let it out, use it! And when people start saying things like "Mary is so wise, so in touch with her feelings, so confident about where she's headed in life," you can either share your little secret . . . or just share a little smile.

TODAY AND TOMORROW
IN TEA LEAVES

For centuries people across the globe have been downing cups of tea simply to gaze into the messy residue and see what their future holds. Although it might seem surprising, this method of divination can be astonishingly accurate. It may be hard to believe that your future could boil down to a handful of tea leaves at the bottom of a cup, but once you learn the knack of deciphering the patterns and symbols, you can unfold a wealth of knowledge.

How do Wiccans use tea leaves in everyday practice? The same way psychics use them, really—to get a peek at what's coming around the bend or to clarify issues that are going on right now. As your Wiccan tea-leaf guru, I will teach you the right and proper way to interpret the leaves and give you a better understanding of how they work. Many people who don't have the know-how tend to misinterpret the symbols at the bottom of a cup and get to thinking that they are doomed to a life of toil and woe, when quite the opposite is true. In this chapter you'll find all the information you need to read the leaves like a pro.

The correct term for this method of divination, which can also be practiced with coffee grounds, is "tasseography" (also known as tasseomancy or tassology). The word comes from the French word *tasse* (cup), which in turn is derived from the Arabic *tassa*. It is believed that tea-leaf readings were first practiced in ancient China and the Middle East, then moved west to Europe along with tea culture before finally reaching the shores of North America.

For some time, tea-leaf readings in the United States were associated with trickery and even thievery. It wasn't until the nineteenth century, with the American Civil War raging, that tea-leaf readings became popular, particularly in the Southern states. Legend has it that soldiers on the way to battle would stop at one of the many plantations along the way to rest, feed their horses, and have a cup of tea, and sometimes a member of the household would offer to tell the soldier his fortune (usually with a positive spin).

VISIONS ARE BREWING

To create visions in your own tea leaves, you have to start cooking. But don't worry; this isn't rocket science or even culinary school.

To begin with, you will need a pot. It doesn't have to be anything fancy, just as long as it boils water. You will also need a white or light-colored cup. This will ensure that you can clearly make out the patterns and images you see in the sediment. The size of the cup is not important, but its width is, as a wider cup bottom will make it easier to see the tea leaves.

Fill the pot with water, put it on the stove, and wait for it to boil. Some people like to use bottled water because they say it's purer. If you don't have this on hand, you can use tap water and bless the pot by saying these words three times:

Cleansed and blessed are thee,
Water pure so mote it be.

Put about half a teaspoon of loose tea leaves in the bottom of the cup. Stir them around while you wait for the water to boil. At this stage, it's important to concentrate on the questions or issues that you want answers to, so focus as best you can and try not to let your mind wander.

When the water in your pot has reached the boiling point, pour it into the cup and stir it for a minute or so, still keeping your mind focused on your questions. Let the tea cool down to a comfortable temperature and then drink it. It's important not to gulp the tea—not only will this give you terrible gas, but you could burn your mouth in the process. Gently strain it through your lips so that you don't drink all of the leaves along with the liquid. (A spittoon nearby could be handy.) It's tricky but worth all the fuss in the end!

When there's just a small amount of liquid left in the bottom of the cup, it's time to stop. Take the cup and swirl the remaining liquid clockwise three times. Put your hand over the top of the cup so you can swoosh the last bit of liquid up the sides without spilling. Now you're ready to read.

TURN OVER A NEW LEAF

Tea-leaf readers from all cultures base their readings on interpreting the shapes formed by the dregs of leaves. When reading the leaves, you are truly getting in touch with your inner self and your subconscious mind. It's very similar to reading the inkblot in a Rorschach test.

Look at the shape created by the leaves. What does it look like to you? Use your imagination to associate a word with it. The first word that comes to mind is very important.

Let's say you asked the teacup if you would be successful in your career. You might imagine that the tea leaves form a car or a train. Tea-leaf reading is similar to dream interpretation in that they both use symbols. However, the

symbols can be interpreted differently because a dream can show movement. For example, in a dream, a parked vehicle would indicate a dead-end or stagnant situation . . . your subconscious mind may be telling you that you are in a dead-end job. But in tea-leaf reading, since the tea leaves are always stationary, you cannot differentiate between movement and non-movement. Most people who see a car associate it with movement, so the subconscious mind would interpret a vehicle symbol as "keep moving forward."

The list is endless when it comes to words, images, and associations, so I will keep it short and simple here to help you get started:

HOUSE: Represents the self; if the house is in good repair, so are you

SHARP OBJECT: Danger

CLOVER: Good luck

CAT: Brief illness

KEY: A new venture is coming

DIAMOND: Expect money from an unexpected source

BIRDS: Good omens

HEART: A reward is coming your way

TRIANGLE: Good karma

SQUARE: Caution!

CIRCLE: Success ahead

NUMBERS: Indicates time in months, days, or years

SNAKE: Wisdom

LEAF: A new lease on life

TELEPHONE: A message is coming

MOUNTAIN: An unfinished task is dogging you

There are dozens of images associated with specific fortunes, and because this subject warrants its own book, I can include only a few here. If you fancy studying this subject at more length, hop on the Internet and look up "tea-leaf reading symbols." This information is readily available to you.

Leanna's Tip

This little secret is rarely talked about in books on reading the tea leaves, but it will help you immensely every time you want to boil up a forecast. Keep a tea-leaf diary on hand whenever you consult the mystical cup. Look at the formations in the leaves. If you see a picture that isn't listed anywhere in your references, meditate on the symbol and use your psychic abilities to find words to represent it. Write down your new findings in your diary so that you can use that interpretation again. Every time you read the oracle, do the same thing. Soon you will be able to combine certain pictures with upcoming events in your life. Within a short time, you'll be predicting your days and events with amazing accuracy!

CHAPTER 17

SHAWN

OH, THE
THINGS
YOU'LL SEE!

HAVE YOU EVER WISHED THAT YOU could sit right where you are, in your comfy chair with a nice cup of tea, and know what's going on with your friends or family who are hundreds of miles away? Some Wiccans actually have the power to home in on the energy of distant places and events, and actually see them, through a skill known as *clairvoyance*. Others hear voices or impressions through *clairaudience* or feel energies through *clairsentience*. These kinds of ESP communications are far more interesting than telephoning your sister who lives down the street, and they're easy to achieve when you know how.

Even though I'm talking about deliberately homing in on people or events that are close to your heart, many Wiccan seers can receive images, sounds, and feelings that they don't necessarily ask for, and often can't control, about people they don't know at all. For these Wiccans (yours truly included), this power can feel like a curse as well as a blessing. First, you can become very burdened with impressions you don't always understand; second, since most ordinary people tend to be skeptical, it is not always easy to get them to heed any warnings you might give them based on your insight.

This is not to say that we seers don't value and appreciate our gifts. We just have to learn to hone them, control them as best we can, and know when and how to put them to good use.

SEERS THROUGH THE CENTURIES

Some believe that religious prophets throughout history received messages from a divine source; others believe that such people were actually receiving messages from the other side. It is possible that these gifted people were receiving some kind of spiritual message that was invisible and inaudible to others. Therefore, it is quite conceivable they possessed some kind of intuitive skill that enabled them to see and hear what wasn't apparent on the physical plane.

Nostradamus (1503–1566), perhaps the most famous seer in history, began his professional life as a physician in France. After his wife and child died of the plague, he fell apart, to be reborn as a teller of the future. He is, of course, the author of the famed book *The Prophecies*, which his followers believe has predicted everything from the assassination of Lincoln to the rise of Hitler to 9/11. Some people question whether Nostradamus was clairvoyant or a

prophet. There's no real scholarly answer to this. As far as I'm concerned, prophets *are* seers, so I would say that he was both.

One famous modern-day American seer was Edgar Cayce (1877–1945), also known as "the sleeping prophet," since many of his visions came to him while he was resting quietly in a trancelike state. When someone with a problem asked Cayce for guidance, the seer would lie down and put himself into a trance and then report his findings to an assistant who was taking notes at his side. Cayce, who believed firmly that the subconscious mind held information not available to the conscious mind, claimed not to remember his visions or what he had told his assistant, but the accuracy of some of his predictions gained him a large following of supporters.

In 1972, researchers Harold Puthoff and Russell Targ conducted a series of studies on remote viewing at the Stanford Research Institute designed to determine whether seers could give precise information about distant locations or persons. Puthoff and Targ chose random locations and then asked the seers to tune in to those spots and either verbally describe or sketch what they were seeing. Three men (including the famed psychic Uri Gellar) were determined to have clairvoyant skills. Of course, some skeptics grumbled and called the experiment a farce, but that is nothing new.

SEE ME, HEAR ME, FEEL ME

Now it's time for us to look at the specifics of receiving remote messages, the different kinds of gifts that are involved, and the various energies that people (including you) may be sensitive to.

CLAIRVOYANTS, as you probably know, receive visions, either while in a state of meditation, while asleep, or while they're going about their daily business.

CLAIRAUDIENTS hear things that are not audible to others. These may be the voices of spirit guides or messages from spirits who have passed.

CLAIRALIENTS can smell the spirit world. For instance, if your deceased grandfather smoked a pipe or ate garlic all the time, you might catch a whiff of pipe tobacco or garlic and know that his spirit is nearby.

CLAIRAMBIENTS can actually taste what a spirit enjoyed during his or her lifetime.

CLAIRSENTIENTS can assess and feel the energetic fields around people and other beings—animals, plants, or anything with a life force—and shift those energies if need be.

CLAIRCOGNIZANTS don't hear or see images, and yet they know things that they couldn't possibly have learned through everyday means. For example, a claircognizant may be able to tell you who your great-great-great-grandfather was, even though he's never heard the man's name before and has no background on your family history. The claircognizant himself doesn't know how this information found its way into his consciousness; it just pops out of his mouth.

For most of this chapter, I'm going to focus on clairvoyance, because that's where my expertise lies. I mention these other abilities because it's not uncommon for seers to have more than one such skill. However, it's also common to have one and be unable to develop another. I know a woman who has been clairaudient since she was a little girl. For years she tried desperately to become clairvoyant, until one day she was wise enough to say to herself, "This is how I receive information, and there's nothing wrong with that!"

LITTLE SEER GIRL

At the beginning of this chapter, I alluded to the fact that I have the gift of clairvoyance. I also implied that this skill has not always been welcome in my life. Let me tell you my story.

My grandmother, an unusual and lovely woman, sat me down one day when I was very young and said, "Shawn, you know you're different, don't you?" I knew that I was, even at that age, but still, because I had no words to describe how I felt or how exactly I was different from other kids, I asked what she meant. She told me I was clairvoyant, explaining, "You know things others don't. You can see things before they happen. You can read what other people are thinking, can't you?"

She was right. I could do all of those things, at least sometimes, but being so young, I thought that everybody could! This was the first time my gifts were laid out on the table before me, so to speak, and I had to acknowledge and accept them as something that set me apart from my friends, something that I had and they didn't.

Just a couple of weeks after this conversation with my grandma, I was playing with my friends when I heard her voice saying good-bye to me, telling me that she'd be seeing me in heaven. You can imagine how upsetting this would be for anyone, let alone a little girl! I ran to my mother and asked what had happened to my grandmother, and I learned that she had been admitted to the hospital. By the end of the day, we got the call that Grandma had passed away.

This is just one of hundreds of messages I've received since my childhood, and that time it was very precise. Other times, though, I've gotten false alarms. I once believed that someone I knew was going to die in a horrible car accident, and I cried and cried and cried all through the day. I found out later that night that she had arrived home safe and sound, and then I had to face the fact that my premonitions weren't always correct. I wasn't sure how I felt about this; I didn't know if I had been flat-out wrong or if I had misinterpreted what I saw, but I was, of course, relieved that she was unharmed.

This kind of misguided intuition can often happen with psychics. Most people have deep-seated fears for their loved ones at one time or another, but when you have the "gift" it is hard to differentiate between your fear and a real message. The psychic wires can get crossed, and then it's easy to lose faith in your ability.

If you have psychic abilities, what should you do when you see something scary or negative in a person's future? Is it helpful to tell the person, or is that something you should keep to yourself? On the one hand, if you can tell the person about something they can likely prevent—like getting hit by a bus—it may be wise to give a warning. On the other hand, if you see long-term illness or extreme sadness, it becomes a little more complicated. Should you tell, or should you just sit there smiling, as if everything were hunky-dory?

Leanna and I are believers in telling the truth, no matter what, but you also have to remember that you are not God and you won't wake up psychic every morning. You have to be tactful and choose your wording very carefully. Also, sometimes the messages we get can be vague or jumbled up, so it's not always the case that you can clearly see your friend or loved one becoming seriously ill or being hit by a bus. Often, you'll just get a message that your friend may need to see a doctor for some reason or that they may experience back pain—nothing too scary to foretell—but later you'll discover how accurate you were when you hear that your friend slipped on ice, hurt their back, and had to see the doctor.

So in the event that you have negative news to report, always be sensitive, and think before you speak. Give a warning without terrifying the life out of your friend or making them feel paranoid, and remember these truths:

* We all have free will. Just because you are seeing something in the future that *could* happen, it doesn't mean that it *will* happen. The future is changing all the time, based on our actions and the actions of other people. It's like the butterfly effect—one small incident can set off a chain reaction of other incidents, so nothing is ever really set in stone.

* The trials in our lives lead us to acquire greater strength and open new doors. Although it does not seem like a good thing at the time, something that seems like a huge tragedy right now—the end of a marriage, the loss of a job—might just be the beginning of a new future. Always give hope and tell people they are learning valuable lessons and being guided by their angels.

* When someone comes to you with a big problem and they have nowhere else to turn, help keep their feet on the ground by telling them that the Divine Creator never gives people anything they can't cope with. Instill your strength into them and encourage them with new ideas.

When you're working with your own skills, it's important to remember that your feelings, and the visions and sound impressions you receive, don't *make* things happen. Nothing you see, hear, or sense will be your fault. The reason I tell you this is that people with powers of ESP sometimes feel very guilty when their negative premonitions come to pass. Sometimes you can warn people, sometimes you can't, and often they won't listen. So take things as they come, use your best judgment as to sharing the information, and then learn to let it go.

HELP US SEE

For all the skepticism surrounding ESP, every now and then you'll hear that a police agency has turned to a clairvoyant for help in cracking a case. Often this is in connection with a missing person, but sometimes a seer will come into a violent crime scene as well.

Seers, whether they consider themselves clairsentient or not, can use, and actually depend on, the energy from the target (in this case, the missing person or the perpetrator) or the crime scene itself to glean valuable information. When I've helped the police solve crimes, I have gone directly into the crime scene. It gives off vibrations that help me to envision what went on there and who might be responsible.

Let me explain how this is possible. When someone commits an act of violence, they leave behind a heap of negative energy. This is kind of like leaving DNA behind, but the authorities can't dust for energy and bag it up like other evidence. If I can connect with that energy, I can get a read on who this person might be, what their current energetic state might be (are they scared? still angry? dead?), and even where they might be. (Do I see or feel a cold, wet, dark place? Might they be in a boathouse or a shipyard?) This is really a form of clairsentience leading me into clairvoyance.

Likewise, when a person has gone missing, it is helpful for the seer to either go to the scene of the abduction (if it's known) or turn to psychometry and to physically hold something that belongs to the person. The item, whatever it is, will help the seer connect to the missing person's current state of energy and perhaps receive a vision of where the person is now.

It frustrates me when I hear skeptics say, "Oh, anyone could give such a vague description of a place!" First, it's better information than any non-seer could provide; second, a vague description is still better than nothing at all, and it does provide some direction for the authorities.

Most seers genuinely want to share their ability to help; most are not out to get famous or to score their own reality shows. They've been born with a skill that, as I said, can feel like a blessing and a curse, and they want the blessings to far outweigh any negativity they've had to deal with.

LEARN TO SEE . . .
WITH YOUR THIRD EYE

Let's say that you suspect you have clairvoyant abilities. How can you develop them? Is there a school for seers? There actually are seminars for sharpening this skill, but you can also try to do it in the privacy of your own home.

Experts in the field will tell you that clairvoyance is the result of having a clear, open "third eye." A little background may be needed if you aren't familiar with the term: the third eye is part of the body's chakra system (see "Swing into Better Health" in chapter 16, pages 238–241). The sixth chakra, location of the third eye, is in the middle of the forehead (though it might be higher or lower on some people); it is related to intuition and a higher understanding of the world.

The first thing you can do to improve your clairvoyance is to make sure that your third-eye chakra is clear. This can be done through a special meditation for which you'll need a blue crystal or a gemstone such as azurite, lapis lazuli, or kyanite.

To begin, dim the lights, light some candles, and put on some music—whatever soothes you. Now lie down and place the blue crystal or stone on your forehead. Breathe deeply—inhale through the nose as deeply as you can, then blow out through the mouth. Breathe in and out this way for thirty to sixty seconds. Start to focus on the area where the crystal is. Imagine the crystal opening up that space. Maybe you'll feel a warming or tingling sensation.

When you're feeling like the space is wide open, make sure you are still breathing deeply. Unfocus your mind (just as we talked about in chapter 13 on scrying) and see whatever comes to you. You don't have to know what the vision is about; you can interpret that part later. For the time being, just be with the vision.

Here's where you can also try to develop clairaudient capabilities. While you're in your deep meditative state, take some time to focus on your ears as well. See if you can hear anything coming to you from the other side.

TELL ME WHAT YOU SEE

Through years of practice and repetition, I've learned how to "call up" visions for other people. If someone comes to me for advice on a particular issue, I can focus enough to "see" what's going to happen.

For example, if a woman came to me asking whether she should keep seeing a certain man, I would close my eyes and enter into a deep meditative or trancelike state while focusing on the question. A date might pop into my mind, in which case I would tell her to mark her calendar and look for something significant to happen; or it might be a location such as a restaurant, in which case I would probably advise her that it could be the site of a significant night on the town with her gentleman friend; or I might actually see a proposal or a breakup.

Like Edgar Cayce, I tend not to remember the trances or what happened during them. A clairvoyant's subconscious mind tends to block out our encounters and leave us with a sense of amnesia. This may be a defense mechanism to keep us from getting overly spooked by things that are unexplained. But I'm always happy to assist whenever and wherever I can, and once you come to develop your ability, I know you will be too!

Leanna's Tip

To enhance your powers of clairvoyance, when you practice, always wear a piece of lapis lazuli (for example, as part of a necklace or a ring) next to the skin. It can also be worn outside of practice to attract visionary vibrations. Once you get into the swing of tapping into your own clairvoyance, visions of forthcoming events will pop into your mind sporadically. Although at first these visions will just seem like your imagination running away with you, you'll gain more confidence in your capabilities once they start coming true.

LEANNA

DOS AND DON'TS ABOUT WITCHCRAFT

These words the Wiccan Rede fulfill:
"An ye harm none, do what ye will."

—from "The Wiccan Rede," anonymous

I'S NOT THAT WE DON'T HAVE THE ABILITY TO HEX our exes or fantasize about turning a particularly insufferable former beloved into a toad! It's simply not ethical, and we don't do it. Most religions follow rules and guidelines, and although Wicca is considered to be a relaxed faith, we also have strict laws that we follow to the letter. Just because we can make magickal things appear out of thin air, it doesn't mean that it's always the right thing to do. It's vital that before we go waving our wands, we think carefully about what we are doing, to make absolutely sure that we are not negatively affecting or hindering another person.

It's true that the majority of witches cast their spells with good intentions, but there are always those who step over the line. There are people the world over who perform black magick because they have been treated badly or are seeking revenge for a wrong. Some are warped with jealousy and wish a bad fate on those more fortunate than themselves, and although it does sound bizarre that in the twenty-first century people are still putting curses on others, it's really not that uncommon. Frankly, these despicable individuals cannot truly call themselves Wiccans, for it is widely understood that witches only work for the greater good. On the other hand, people who use these skills to do harm are just self-interested souls who use magick as a way of gaining control and power over others, using it purely for their own gratification.

An inexperienced witch may sometimes delve into the dark side without actually meaning to. Once upon a time, when I wasn't the sweet, kind witch I am today, I purposely cast the evil eye on my neighbor. For as long as I could remember, she had been a really dislikeable character who for some reason looked down her nose at our family. She would complain to us about almost anything—from our cats to overhanging branches from our trees—and would constantly gossip about us to other neighbors. After endless attempts at biting my tongue and being polite, something inside me flipped. One day, she was so rude to me that I forgot all my manners, looked her straight in the eye, and under my breath wished a plague of locusts on her. Of course, the plague of locusts didn't miraculously appear out of the sky and swarm toward her, but a few minutes after I muttered those fateful words, the handbrake on her car snapped and the car proceeded to roll down the hill. Luckily, she and her passengers had already gotten out, so there were no casualties, but her automobile did crash into another neighbor's front porch, causing a lot of damage.

My mother took me aside and raised that wise old eyebrow of hers. She said quietly, "You do realize that was your fault!" I had to admit that, at the tender age of fifteen, my powers and thought projection were getting stronger by the day. As you can imagine, my mother was further horrified when I just shrugged my shoulders and laughed a wicked adolescent laugh. Because I had broken the first rule of Wicca—"Harm none"—she grounded me for a week. Most kids back then got grounded for staying out late or getting drunk, whereas I was imprisoned for hexing my neighbor. It didn't end there, though, because shortly afterward, karmic forces intervened. Our automobile broke down on a country lane and needed extensive repairs. So the nasty thought I'd sent out to my neighbor bounced right back and bit us.

HOW POWERFUL IS THE MIND?

You don't need to set up an altar with half a dozen bat's feet and thirteen black candles on it in order to curse someone. A simple thought of hatred toward another person can have the same effect. When we think a thought with feeling, we are in fact hurling an energy ball into the ether. Scientists have not yet fully explored the mysteries of this power, but just as we can do damage with our bodies, we can also cause injuries with our minds. A mental hex—called the "evil eye" in many cultures across the world—is widely feared.

By targeting an individual and sending fiendish thoughts their way, we can create a negative energy that hovers like a black cloud over them and sometimes their loved ones too. Life for them becomes stressful and difficult and often spirals out of control. Illness may befall them, financial hardship may hit, they may lose their jobs, or other terrible things may happen to them. Only strong-minded people with a little bit of magickal know-how recognize this negativity and know how to stop it from reaching them. Although you can protect yourself with pentacles, salt, prayers of protection from angels, and other methods, these techniques only work if you have the strength of mind to believe that the curse will not reach you, because negativity thrives on fear. I haven't made many enemies in my life, but on the very few occasions that I have, I've noticed a certain level of chaos building up in my everyday life. This can be anything from the roof needing repairs to a pet getting sick to catching a very bad cold. It's at times like these that I block destructive thoughts, which deflects them straight back to the sender.

It's not always easy to be pure of heart, because we are human beings and we were born to be emotional. People often make us furious, and it's one of our basic instincts to seek revenge if someone does us a wrong. If, for whatever reason, you find yourself despising or loathing someone, you have to rise above those natural instincts and be the better man or woman.

The best way is to avoid mixing with individuals who hinder your soul and to remove those people from your life completely if you can. It's important that the people around you connect perfectly with your own energy, complementing it rather than disrupting it. If this isn't possible— say, you have to see your ex-partner every weekend when he or she visits the kids—try your utmost to be civil and courteous and keep telling yourself that you're the better person. Self-control is a wonderful thing, and although you may not feel very godly at the time, you'll feel better once you realize you have not increased your negative karmic load. By being the very best you can be, you redress the imbalance in the situation. It shows great strength of character and acts as a way to further your spiritual development. Your guides and angels commend this type of behavior and often throw in a little reward to follow, be it a bit of extra cash or just a wonderful day out.

WHAT SHOULD YOU DO IF YOU THINK SOMEONE HAS CURSED YOU?

I get many letters with questions from my readers, and this has to be the most commonly asked question of all. Usually, if you are free of enemies, then it's unlikely that the bad luck you are encountering has anything to do with a hex. However, if you don't get along that well with your mother-in-law, or if your ex-husband is bad-mouthing you at every opportunity, then it's quite possible that their negativity is affecting you in some way. Therefore, it's essential that you keep your enemies to a minimum. If there is someone who clearly doesn't like you, then you need to either try and make that relationship better or remove yourself from it—period. If you are not in their face 24/7, then they will not be silently cursing you all the time and causing you problems.

Sometimes it's not that easy, though, and for whatever reason, life will make sure we are in the same vicinity as our enemies on a regular basis. In situations where it's impossible to move away from a person, spells such as the ones below are sometimes necessary to keep negative vibes from being launched in your direction.

MIRROR MAGICK

In my opinion, the mirror is one of the most commanding items in the witch's protective tool kit. Gather together as many small mirrors as you can find and place one facing outward in every window of your home. (If you have multipaned windows, there is no need to place a mirror in every pane; one is quite sufficient.) The mirror will reflect any negative vibes, bouncing them right back to where they came from so they don't interrupt the balance of your life. It will create a protective force field to keep you free from trouble and strife. I keep my mirrors in place at all times, only removing them for a quick dusting before I put them right back.

SWEETEN THAT SOUL

For a bit of extra energy, and to add to the magick of the mirror, why not try casting a spell to sweeten your enemy's mood? This is a great way to build up your positive karma, and it guarantees that he or she will be sending you nicer thoughts in the future. Take a piece of letter-size paper and, with a black pen, write your name and underneath it your foe's name. Take two pink rose petals and a pinch of salt and place them in the middle of the paper. These items represent harmony and cleansing and will magickally calm down antagonism. Fold the paper in half (make sure the petals remain inside the paper). Then fold the paper once more in half. Keep folding the paper until you cannot fold it anymore. Once you have folded it until it is as small as it can be, place it on a table and light a yellow candle next to it. Say the following spell three times:

> Angels bless this soul,
> Make our union pleasant,
> Calm their disposition,
> Evil thoughts be absent.
> So mote it be.

The candle should be left to burn down and extinguish itself.

FOCUS ON YOUR HOCUS-POCUS

Of course, no spell is going to work if you don't have faith in your own abilities. The craft is all about sending out positive intentions, so if you are in the middle of a spell and you begin doubting whether or not it is going to work, it's unlikely that it will. Getting yourself in the right frame of mind is all-important. You have to trust in your power and believe wholeheartedly that you will succeed. If you happen to have little nagging doubts entering your brain every few seconds, then you must try and banish them. A good way to do this is to keep telling yourself that your spell *will* work. Once you have succeeded with a few spells and have seen the results firsthand, you will naturally develop a confidence in your craft, but in the early days, novice witches need to focus, focus, focus!

It's a bit like going for a job interview and sitting nervously in reception, waiting to be called in. If you tell yourself you have no hope of winning the job, then you probably won't. However, if you walk in there with confidence blazing and project the right attitude, you may just walk out triumphant. It's actually the same with spell casting. I have no doubt that each and every one of my spells will work. So much so that on the odd occasion when a spell doesn't have the desired effect, I'm quite shocked!

WHEN A SPELL DOES A NOSEDIVE

When a spell seems not to have the desired effect, you can try doing it again, but sometimes things happen for a reason and no amount of spell casting can change a situation. I think our guides and angels help us whenever they can, but every now and then we are faced with situations for one simple reason, and that is for the purpose of learning. It may be that we are not allowed to sweeten our boss's mood because we have to learn to stand up for ourselves. Victims of life are often surrounded by strong-minded individuals and will continue to be until they fight for respect. If this is the case, your bullying boss or your controlling mother-in-law will not let up until you put your foot down once and for all.

On the other hand, your spells could be failing because you are tired or sick. Your aura has to be in tip-top condition if your spell is to succeed, so before you begin any magick, make sure that you have not just had a fight with your partner, screamed at your children for dropping popcorn all over the floor, or started running a fever.

Many witches will meditate for half an hour or so before venturing into any spell casting. Some stare into flames while trying to clear their minds of daily hustles and bustles. Quiet reflection soothes the soul and helps us to generate a calm and peaceful ambience.

GO ORGANIC

Mother Earth is a wonderful thing, and when we look at our planet in its natural state—without human interference—everything sits in perfect balance. The laws of nature should be respected and appreciated, and because we are just visitors to this planet, we should try not to deface it in any way. Witches believe that we have a duty to our earth, and although I don't believe in going overboard, if we all became a little "greener" and looked after our own tiny corner of the world, we wouldn't have as many global problems as we have today.

I am lucky because I live on a farm in the heart of southwestern England, and people who have visited here from afar say it's like stepping back in time somewhat. Although living in the middle of a rural field does have its problems, I am fortunate enough to have the space to grow all my own fruits and vegetables and be as organic as the slugs allow.

Believe it or not, all foods have a negative or positive vibration. This is important to know, because every time you bite into a ham-and-cheese sandwich or lick the cream from a chocolate éclair, that food has come from some source somewhere. If the pig that is now in your sandwich was an unhappy pig (let's say that his living conditions resembled those of a Siberian prison), the energy you are putting into your body is negative energy.

Food and water are our fuel and sustenance. In order to function properly on a day-to-day basis, in mind, body, and spirit, we have to look at food as our gasoline. You wouldn't put diesel in an unleaded car, so why put the wrong fuel in your body? Let's face it, your body has to carry you around for the rest of your life, so it's necessary that you give it the right fuel, service it regularly, and change the oil from time to time. I fully appreciate that not everyone can grow their own food in their backyard and that most of us are slaves to the supermarket shelves, but try to eat a balanced, nutritious diet and buy free-range meat and eggs and organic produce when you can. This will help ensure that your aura and your energy remain well adjusted.

GREEDY WITCHES CAUSE MAGICKAL GLITCHES

Some witches think that casting a spell for money is the biggest sin you can commit, but I just shrug my shoulders and wish them well in their poverty. Money does make the world go round, and summoning a little extra to make life easier never hurts.

It's funny how money magick works, because you don't encounter many rich witches. There are never copious amounts of currency stashed away in our bank accounts, and we rarely drive around in fancy cars—that would be all too easy! This is because, when we conjure the cash, we are only allowed to receive exactly what we need. Therefore it is always best to be specific about the amount you require; you never know, you may just get it. Believe me, if I could grab my wand and zap up a winning lottery ticket, I would, but unfortunately, there are unwritten rules and regulations, and so far I have never heard of someone becoming a multimillionaire as a result of spell casting.

We may have established that you will never be a well-off witch or a wealthy warlock through casting spells, but all is not completely lost. You can actually make some magick to increase the size of your purse and pay for those little extras. The best way to do this is to inscribe your name and the amount of money you need on a clean green candle. Place it near something electric, such as a television or kettle, as this will amplify the magick and make it work more quickly. Light the candle and say this incantation seven times:

> *The money I need is for good and not greed.*

Close by saying:

> *So mote it be.*

As always, let the candle burn down and go out on its own. Over the next few days you may start receiving little cash injections, possibly from unexpected sources. Now comes the important part. Always give a small portion of your magickal money back to society. It doesn't really matter who or what you give it to, just as long as you do. If you fail to circulate some of the cash, then the total amount that you received will be whisked away from you in the future. So let's say that after you've cast your spell you unexpectedly receive $100. Take $5 and put it in a charity box. This guarantees that you keep the remaining $95, and everyone benefits!

MAGICKAL MEDDLING

People ask me all the time to bring back lovers who have packed their suitcases and left, or to make the sexy guy in the next office fall hopelessly in love with them, and my answer each and every time is "No!" It is not our right to interfere or influence the way a person thinks or feels. Witches believe that everyone has the free will to love whomever they want and it is not our place to meddle in such affairs. Love and romance play a large part in everybody's lives, and it is only natural that people will want to ensure they are as happy as they can be in those areas, but there are some things that it is just not right to do. However, there is so much to say about the issue of love magick that we have devoted a whole chapter to it (see chapter 10), so for now, let's finish with an important set of guidelines that every witch should keep in mind when spell casting.

1. ALWAYS ENSURE THAT NO OTHER PERSON WILL BE HARMED AS A RESULT OF YOUR MAGICK. To call yourself a witch means that you will always endeavor to do the right thing and send out only love and kindness to others. Think about The Wizard of Oz and strive to be like the Good Witch of the North. Glinda managed it, and so can you!

2. KEEP YOUR THOUGHTS FREE OF NEGATIVITY—REMEMBER THE REBOUND EFFECT. Keep in mind that every thought you send out can just as easily bounce off the receiver and be hurled back at you at the speed of light. You created the negative fog, so it belongs to you!

3. NEVER CAST A SPELL WHEN YOU ARE UPSET OR UNHEALTHY. Funny as it may seem, our thought projections can go haywire if we are cross, unhappy, or sick. Spells may fail to work, or the results may be confusing. Therefore it's imperative that we be in the right frame of mind and physically healthy before we begin any magick.

4. THINK POSITIVELY. If you smile, then you are more likely to be happy. Every time a miserable thought pops into your head, shake it away

and try to think about something nice. Your aura is a magnetic energy field, and if it's drab or gloomy, you will attract disruptive and depressing situations.

5. CREATE A PEACEFUL, CALM ENVIRONMENT FOR SPELL CASTING. Make your space as lovely as possible with candles, soft music, and lots of salt at hand to ward off negativity. Keep your home free of clutter and clean house regularly.

6. CALL UPON YOUR ANGELS TO ASSIST YOU. Your angels are never far away, and they will gladly help and support you when you are trying to change a situation. Before casting your spell, say a silent prayer to the angelic forces for protection and you'll be sure to envelop yourself in their influence.

7. RESPECT EVERYTHING. There is no need to be obsessive, especially if you are feeling the financial pinch, but try as hard as you can to eat all the right foods. Food is fuel and it affects your aura, so be as organic as you can. Eat badly and you'll feel bad. Bear in mind that every animal, vegetable, and leaf has a spirit, so treat everything with the respect it deserves.

8. WISH FOR MONEY BUT BE CAREFUL OF GREED. If you need to cast spells for material gain, then make sure that when you receive money as a result of magick, you give a little away to keep the cycle of good fortune going. A dollar in a charity box is quite enough; as long as you spread the wealth, your karma will stay positive.

9. NEVER INFLUENCE A PERSON'S MIND WITH MAGICK. Everyone deserves the right to free will, so *never* cast a spell to influence a person's decisions. Doing so has drastic consequences. You could indirectly take that person off the path they are destined to travel and deprive

them of lessons they need to learn. If you cast a spell to win back an ex, for example, it may be that you've derailed their fated union with somebody else in the future. If you've reeled them back in, you have interfered with their karma, and you could get your karmic wrist slapped when you eventually pass over into spirit.

10. BELIEVE IN YOURSELF. No amount of magick will work unless you have faith in yourself, so make sure that you truly believe in your spells. Then success will be yours.

Shawn's Tip

Understand that everything happens for a reason, so if your spell doesn't work, don't beat yourself up. Before you go to sleep, ask your angels to give you a wider understanding of why you can't have what you want; you may find that the answers come along in dream sleep.

SHAWN

DESTINY IS CALLING YOU

HERE COMES A TIME WHEN ONE HAS TO ASK: what is this merry-go-round of life all about? I'm not going to lie and tell you that as Wiccans we know all the answers, because we don't. What we do know is that we all have the ability to engage with and use the energy around us, and this blessing can be passed on to enrich and change lives, including your own. It is a power far greater than the mind can imagine, and what you do with this power can change the course of your destiny and touch the lives of others as well.

When you are walking your path of life and suddenly feel lost, you have to rely upon your sixth sense, the omnipotent power that sees, hears, and knows all. It is perfectly safe to flip the switch on your ancient instincts and look beyond closed doors—or doors that you *believed* were closed, anyway—but be aware that the ability to see what others cannot may leave you feeling drained.

Witches tend to be very empathetic people. Some of us even call ourselves empaths, as we mentioned at the start of this book, since we have the ability to literally feel the emotions and energy emanating from others. When you walk around picking up feelings from strangers on the street, it can often feel like an immense burden, because you're dealing with everyone's issues and problems. You can allow these feelings to drag you into a deep depression, or you can try to shield yourself and instead look for ways to work for the greater good.

We know that it's all but impossible to help everyone on a personal basis, but it's important to help those who seek you out to the best of your ability. As for the rest of the world, believe it or not, there *are* ways to help the people you don't know and may never meet!

ONE-ON-ONE HELP

Helping individual people in Wiccan ways isn't a hard thing to do. It is just the same as if you were an accountant and someone asked you to help them with their taxes. You have a certain set of skills that you can put to good use fairly easily, and one of the rarer skills may be communicating with souls who have crossed over or gotten "stuck" on their way to the other side.

Let's say that you have a friend who has suffered the loss of a loved one and it seems the deceased person is not at peace. It's not uncommon for a soul to become "lost" or confused when their death was especially sudden or traumatic; some can hang around the earth plane for centuries, believing that they are still alive or that they still have business to attend to.

There are plenty of ways for the living to help a dead soul's transition to the spiritual realm, and when you do so, you're actually helping your friend *and* the spirit. Here are some things you can try (after first protecting your aura as outlined on pages 280–281:

PRAYERS: If your friend is religious, pray with them for the soul of the deceased to make a peaceful passage to the next world. (It doesn't really matter if you believe in the power of prayer or not—you're helping your friend just by engaging in the ritual with them.)

SPIRIT GUIDES: These are "helper souls" on the other side. To make contact, close your eyes, quiet your mind, and offer up a simple "Hello?" in your thoughts—and then listen for a response. As we have mentioned in previous chapters, some people can actually see and hear their spirit guides. For your purposes here, you want to ask the spirit guide to intervene and lead the trapped soul to the spirit realm.

MEDITATION AND VISUALIZATION: Take your friend's hand and guide them through a visualization in which you imagine leading the deceased soul by the hand down a beautiful garden path. Leave the friend and the deceased to walk the last hundred feet of the path alone. Before you do this exercise, your friend can prepare a "pep talk" of sorts encouraging the spirit to pass on to the next world. They can say their good-byes at the end of the path.

LIGHTING A WHITE CANDLE: White candles represent pureness and light. As the wick burns and smoke begins to rise, meditate and visualize the spirit of the deceased also rising and evaporating from this world.

Use your intuition to decide which method will work best, or use a pendulum to help you make the call, but make sure to engage your powers of intention to help you help the spirit. Without it, you're just going through the motions, and that confused soul isn't going *anywhere*.

FINDING THOSE IN NEED

Assisting friends and loved ones is sometimes an easy thing to do—they come to us asking for advice, and we can often intuit exactly what they need. But there are others out there who could use a helping hand too. Sometimes we know them personally (a sick relative two thousand miles away), sometimes we don't (victims of natural disasters around the globe), but as Wiccans, we can feel a pull on our energy, that sense of "I wish I could do something to help!" How do we help those we can't be with, those who can't come to us for a reading or a spell? There are some things we can do as individuals, or as small groups, including:

MEDITATION: Whether you meditate alone or with a like-minded group, you can send out vibes for world peace, better health for those afflicted by illness, an improved economy, jobs for the unemployed, you name it. The intention is what's important here, whether or not you know who specifically will benefit from your work.

DONATIONS: This sounds simple, but so many of us either forget that there are those in need or just give without thinking. Again, your intention is of the utmost importance here. It's easy to toss a donation envelope in the mail and be done with it. Next time, try attaching a positive intention to that donation. Everyone indirectly uses pen-and-paper magick when they send blessings on a birthday card, for instance, so pop a note inside wishing the recipient luck and success with their venture. This will carry a hidden spark of magick.

FOCUSED INTENTION: When you see people on the street who look like they've just lost their best friend, take a second to focus positive energy and send it their way. They may never know what you've done for them, but hopefully it will break through their field of sadness and touch them in some way.

SPELLS FOR HEALING: There are several spells you can perform to invoke healing in a broad sense, that is, to call for peace and harmony in the lives of many people instead of focusing on the well-being of one friend or family member. Here's one: Place five blue candles in a large circle on the ground. On a blank sheet of paper, write the word *peace*. Now light the candles and seat yourself in the middle of the circle, focusing your vision and your thoughts on that word. Breathe deeply as you visualize all good things coming to those who need them most.

BURN AWAY THE NEGATIVITY: There are several Wiccan ceremonies that involve burning words written on slips of paper as an offering to the heavens. Try this one: On small pieces of paper, write the things you'd like to see changed in the world around you, then place them in an ashtray or some other container you can burn things in. The things you write might be similar to the goals we discussed for meditation above—perhaps you'd like to see war, disease, and poverty wiped out. Now focus your intention by visualizing the world the way you dream it could be. When you're ready, light the pieces of paper and watch the negativity burn away. Breathe deeply and have confidence that your intention will make a difference.

This burning practice is often performed in group ceremonies as a means to help right the wrongs in the world, and to make the world a more peaceful place to live. So if you can gather a group of peaceful-minded people (they don't have to be Wiccans, just men and women full of positive intentionality), you can have an even greater impact. Just be careful to always start any focused intention, meditation, or spell with a visualization of protection and then also cleanse your energetic field afterward.

PROTECTING YOUR AURA

Throughout this book, when we've talked about spells and meditations and psychic skills, we've thrown in some warnings about protecting yourself from dark spirits. Since we want you to use your powers to their fullest and not be afraid to tune in to them, we are including some tips for keeping your spiritual aura as clean and as guarded as possible.

First of all, in general, keep yourself physically and emotionally healthy. Eat nutritious foods and follow a balanced diet. Avoid excessive alcohol and drugs. Drink plenty of water and get lots of rest. Exercise regularly, whether it is a brisk walk or a gym workout. Try to keep your outlook on life as positive as you can. These are just commonsense suggestions. It's easier for negative entities to invade a body that has a few chinks in its armor, so to speak.

Second, try these more specific ways of protecting yourself:

* Before you begin a spell, meditation, visualization, or any type of psychic reading, sit down in a comfortable spot. Close your eyes and breathe deeply. Envision a white light in front of you or above you, stretching out to envelop you completely. (White light is *the* protective element of psychics and mediums.) Candles, when lit, attract a higher form of spiritual vibration; they are known to ward off evil spirits, so have one nearby and light it before you begin working.

* Keep garlic on hand—dark spirits really do hate it!

* Use those spirit guides. Call on them and ask them for protection.

* Wear an amulet to ward off evil energy. If you don't have an amulet, they're easy enough to find—in fact, many are natural elements, and things like stones, flowers, bones, and four-leaf clovers will all work beautifully. Quartz crystals also make for powerful amulets. Now, I know you want to ask, "So you're telling me that I can just go out and pick a flower and it will protect me from nasty, dark beings?" The answer here is yes and no. The flower can only protect you if you infuse it with your intention. There are some pretty involved rituals for doing this, but I believe that you can accomplish the same thing simply by meditating with the object for several minutes. Hold it in your hand and try a simple chant, such as "I ask the power of nature to protect me from all malevolent spirits."

* Make a talisman, which is a stronger protector than an amulet. To do this, you have to combine several materials or elements and infuse them with the same intention as above. The difference is that talismans (unlike amulets) sometimes contain materials that you won't find in the woods, such as metal, or even elements that have particular meaning to the wearer, such as a lucky penny. Protective gemstones for talismans include tiger's eye, clear quartz, diamond, hematite, turquoise, and Apache's tear. Dendritic opal (sometimes called merlinite) is also a good stone for magick.

* One last thing—to cleanse yourself after a ritual or reading, soak in a bath containing equal parts sea salt and baking soda. Usually a teaspoon of each dissolved in a tub of warm water is quite sufficient. The combination helps to wash off any negativity that may have attached itself to you.

Talismans

A pebble talisman is quite powerful. To make one, take a small pebble and leave it in salt water overnight to cleanse it. The next day, take the pebble out to dry. Once it has dried, write your wish on the pebble with a permanent marker and place it in a pouch along with one or more of the other gemstones mentioned in the list above. Carry your talisman pouch with you to attract good fortune.

PROTECTION FOR YOUR HOME OR WORKSPACE

Wiccans need to feel free to create and practice spells, divination, meditation, contact with spirit guides, and more. Some amazing things will come to you in your work; the downside, of course, is that there are some nasty spirits out there as well, and they can make their way into our world if we leave the door open, so to speak. By keeping yourself healthy and protected (using the methods we've talked about in this chapter), you can keep dark spirits from invading your body; however, you also want to keep them from setting up shop in your home. Keep the energy in the space where you perform spells or practice divination as clear and clean as possible using these methods:

* Wind chimes and bells are good repellents of negative energies. So hang some chimes outside your door and keep a bell on hand whenever

you're working on a spell, making contact with the spirit world, or peering into the future.

* Burning basil, rosemary, or sage keeps foul spirits away. These herbs are easy to find, obviously, which is why I list them first, but frankincense, lavender, myrrh, mandrake, or valerian root will give you the same results. Sandalwood and rose incense are also great protectors against evil, and they have an added bonus—they make your house smell like you've done some cleaning. Simply scatter the herbs around your work space. To make them into a fine powder (unnoticeable to the human eye), put them in your coffee grinder; then you can sprinkle your space with herb dust. The protective nature of these herbs can also be activated by burning a small amount of them in a bowl in your work space.

* Smudge your space and your aura every now and then. No, I don't mean that you should wipe your hands all over the walls. Get yourself a smudge stick (dried sage, cedar, sweet grass, or lavender—you can find these at a metaphysical shop or online). Set your intention—to cleanse the area and yourself—and then light the stick. The smoke wipes out the negative energy, so really get into the corners and wave it all around.

* When you are chilling out in front of the TV at night, light a pretty-colored scented candle. Any type is fine. Candles are simply great at cleansing an area and will leave the energies balanced and intact.

* As always, before you get into any reading or spell, focus on a positive intention. Envision a white light encircling the entire room you're working in. Call on spirit guides to keep the area clear of evil. Ask and ye shall receive, my friend.

GO FORTH AND DO SOME GOOD

I hear people bad-mouth Wiccans all the time. Unfortunately, if you are open about your beliefs and practices, you're bound to catch some flak, because there are still some old-fashioned and uneducated individuals out there. Most Wiccans take it all with a grain of salt, because we know deep down that we are in fact good people.

We know that everyone is born with certain talents. Some people are naturally athletic; some can sing like rock stars; some are dancers, poets, or mathematical geniuses. If you heard that a child who was a whiz at numbers wasn't using his gifts because his friends and family thought it was a strange inclination, you'd probably think, "What a shame. He could do so much with that talent!" It's just as sad when intuitive boys, girls, men, and women shut down or ignore their abilities. There are skeptics out there who will tell you that witches are fake or troubled in some way, that spell casting and divination are a bunch of bunk, and that you should distance yourself from this stuff as much as possible. This, more than anything else, is the reason people shut down their abilities. They're fearful of society's reactions, of what their families will say and what their friends might think.

This is what we think: when your destiny calls, you have to answer—and just by virtue of the fact that you have read this book, I'd say you've got destiny on the line! So acknowledge the Wiccan gifts that you've been given. There are many, many ways for you to get out there and use what you've got, and just as many ways for you to help people who need it. And when you can do that, I think you'll find that your skills will sharpen and your powers will open up even wider. Remember, it's in giving that we receive, and even though life may throw a heap of trouble at you from time to time, you cannot teach what you haven't learned.

Shawn and Leanna's Final Tip

Be confident. Be loving. Be kind. Be the very best that you can be. We promise it will come back to you threefold.

SPECIAL
ACKNOWLEDGMENTS TO...

Bill Gladstone, our literary agent at Waterside Productions. Thank you for your vision and foresight and belief in the two witches the universe sent to you from opposite sides of the pond.

Barbara Berger, our editor at Sterling Publishing. We send her the Golden Broom Award for believing in us and making our book come true! Special thanks also to Christine Heun, for the beautiful design, and to Hannah Reich, Sterling project editor.

—*Shawn*

A very big thank you to my friend and original editor Karol Kowalczyk, who painstakingly pored over every word of this book. Without his help and attention to detail, I'm sure *Wiccapedia* would not possess the magick it does now.

—*Leanna*

GLOSSARY

ALTAR A base to work from while performing spells and rituals. It can be a coffee table, a shelf, or even a cloth on the floor.

AMETHYST A lavender-purple crystal used for healing or to help calm nerves.

ANGELICA ROOT An herb used for summoning angels and invoking protection.

ANGELIC WICCA A newer branch of witchcraft based on angel energy.

ANOINTING CANDLES To anoint a candle, dip your finger into a tiny drop of oil and run your finger around the base of the candle prior to lighting it.

ASTRAL PROJECTION The ability to release your spirit from your body during a trancelike state, so your spirit can leave the earthly plane temporarily and enter a different reality.

ATHAME A ceremonial knife, typically black-handled with a double-edged blade, used for casting magickal circles before commencing a spell.

BASIL An herb used for attracting wealth and prosperity and aiding fertility.

BAY An herb used in magickal practices to facilitate lucid dreaming.

BELL An item usually present in the witch's tool kit; used for banishing bad vibes.

BESOM A round-bottomed broomstick symbolizing fertility; used by female witches in fertility rites and to sweep away negativity.

BOOK OF SHADOWS A journal or diary witches use for jotting down and recording their spells.

CANDLES Candles represent the elements fire and air. Most spells include at least one candle.

CATNIP An herb carried in one's purse or pocket to attract love and popularity or to be safe when traveling. Often given to friends as a way of sealing friendships.

CHAKRAS Seven spirals of energy located on the ethereal body and said to be connected to the vital organs of the physical body.

CHALICE Symbolizes fertility; in times past, its bowl represented the womb of the goddess, the base of the vessel signified our earthly world, and the stem suggested human rapport with the spirits.

CHAMOMILE An herb used in magickal practices to cure insomnia.

CHARGING Leaving an object such as a pentacle outside overnight (or on your front porch or window ledge) during a full moon phase, to cleanse and bless the object and imbue it with magickal energy.

CHIVES An herb hung high above the front door to keep out unwanted spirits.

CINNAMON BARK Used in spells to attract wealth and increase psychic ability.

CITRINE A crystal representing abundance, good luck, and inspiration.

CLOVES A kitchen spice that can be used with certain spells. Cloves pushed into oranges can help find true love and bring an end to grieving.

COMFREY LEAF Used in spells to settle emotions and for travel protection.

COVEN A group of Wiccan followers who share their spells and rituals and unite to perform communal magick, using their collective energy to give the spells more power.

DANDELION A plant used to summon spirits or assist in health spells.

DARK OF THE MOON A three-day phase immediately before a new moon; considered to be the most magickal and potent of all the moon phases.

DILL An herb used by witches to protect children.

DIVINATION The use of tools, cards, and psychic insight to predict the future.

EARTH ANGELS Angels who take on human form and who are designated to live among people on Earth to help them in times of need.

ECHINACEA An herb applied in spells to ward off colds and flu and to aid healing.

ELDERBERRIES AND ELDERFLOWERS Herbs given to a bride on her wedding day to make sure she remains protected and happy in her marriage.

EUCALYPTUS An herb used as a disinfectant, for balancing emotions, and to make decisions.

FAMILIARS A familiar is a Wiccan's animal companion that supports a witch by aiding her magickal work.

FEVERFEW An herb renowned for getting rid of headaches.

FRANKINCENSE An aromatic resin used for assisting any health spells.

GARLIC Hung by witches in doorways to ward off evil. Also, garlic salt is put into pouches and sachets to keep away bad vibrations.

GUIDES ("WHITE LIGHTERS") Souls who have more or less completed their incarnations. They have lived endless lives, have learned countless lessons, have gone on to "graduate," and are designated to help humans along their journey of life.

HANDFASTING An ancient pagan wedding ceremony practiced by witches, using cords or ribbons to bind the hands together.

HEATHER A lucky herb to have in the home. When hung in a window, it is said to bring good fortune to the inhabitants.

HEMATITE A shiny black, slate-gray, or silvery-red mineral used for safety during astral travel and then for grounding once the spirit returns to the body.

HIGH PRIEST/HIGH PRIESTESS A high-ranking clergy who heads a coven and performs handfastings.

INCANTATION A rhyming spell, usually spoken repeatedly during a ritual.

INCENSE Sticks of dried herbs, spices, or resins used in magickal practices to cleanse areas and invoke universal energies.

INSCRIBING Using a knife or pin to scratch wishes into the wax of a candle.

LAPIS LAZULI A rich blue stone used to ward off negative vibrations.

LAVENDER Lavender is incorporated into spell casting for calming and to promote peaceful sleep.

MANDRAKE ROOT An herb used widely by witches to give spells more power.

MINT A garden herb used in rituals to help summon angels.

MISTLETOE A seasonal plant used magickally in wish boxes and sachets for love and fertility.

MOLDAVITE A rare and precious crystal, thought to be extraterrestrial, formed from the impact of a meteor hitting Earth.

MOONSTONE A mystical crystal used to encourage premonitions during dreams, as well as to calm volatile energies.

MUGWORT An herb used to boost a spell's performance.

NETTLE A garden weed employed by witches to drive out unwanted spirits.

NUMEROLOGY A divination system that assigns meaning to numbers in order to help predict the future and intuit information about a person's character.

OAK BARK Used magickally to raise energy levels and increase emotional strength.

OPIUM A plant used in incense to induce sleep and invigorate psychic senses.

OUIJA BOARD A board with the letters of the alphabet imprinted onto it and the words "yes" and "no." Used to summon spirits during séances.

PENDULUM A weighted object that is swung from a string or chain and used during dowsing—a form of divination witches practice for divining truth, balancing energy, cleansing chakras, or making contact with the spirit realm.

PENTACLE A five-pointed star, known as both a pentacle and a pentagram, and believed to date back more than five thousand years to ancient Mesopotamia. The five points represent the five elements; spirit is the topmost point, and the other points, moving in a clockwise direction, are water, fire, earth, and air.

POPPY SEEDS Used in pouches for love and fertility spells.

PSYCHIC Having extrasensory sensitivity and perception and an ability to divine the future. Comes from the Greek word *psychikos*, meaning "of the soul."

PSYCHOMETRY The ability to hold an object that belongs to someone else as a way to assess the person's character and future.

QUARTZ A multipurpose crystal that can be included in almost any spell to bring about a positive result.

ROSEMARY One of the most widely used herbs in Wicca, rosemary is good for the soul and is a powerful cleanser.

ROSE QUARTZ A crystal relating to all things romantic, used to attract a beloved in spellcraft.

SAGE An herb often used in the form of a smudging stick or as incense to cleanse and purify an area. Also thought to promote wisdom and knowledge.

SAINT-JOHN'S-WORT An herb used for protection against fire, to banish ghosts and demons, and for promoting psychic vision.

SALT A fantastic source of protection used in many spells to banish anything evil.

SANDALWOOD An herb used to ease distress.

SCRYING A way of "seeing" spiritual visions and foretelling the future by looking into a reflective or mutable surface of some kind.

SPELL A form of cosmic ordering or thought projection. A ritual using a collection of objects and tools.

TALISMANS Objects or charms that are charged with energy in order to bring about good fortune and good luck or that are used for specific purposes, such as to enhance fertility.

TEA LEAF READINGS A method of divination using tea leaves in a cup.

TURQUOISE A gemstone employed by witches to ward off the evil eye or protect against negative people or negative influences.

VALERIAN A plant whose leaves or dried roots can be placed in wish boxes to ease tension and arguments. Also used in animal spells.

VERVAIN An herb carried by witches to increase cash flow or improve one's career.

WAND For spell-casting purposes, the wand is used as a summoning tool and also to bless and charge objects.

WICCA An open-minded, nature-loving faith that can be fine-tuned to suit one's needs.

WISH BOX Any size box with a lid; traditionally filled with herbs or spices. Used in conjunction with a spell to invoke one's wish.

WHITE LIGHTERS See "Guides."

YLANG-YLANG Flowers from the ylang-ylang tree, often used in incense, that can enhance love spells, harmonize marriages, and heal impotence.

INDEX

Note: Page numbers in **bold** indicate glossary terms.

(*continued*)

PICTURE CREDITS